the
shock
of your
life

D0542229

the shock of your life

ADRIAN HOLLOWAY

KINGSWAY PUBLICATIONS
EASTBOURNE

Copyright © Adrian Holloway 2000

The right of Adrian Holloway to be identified
as author of this work has been asserted by him
in accordance with the Copyright, Designs
and Patents Act 1988.

First published 2000
Reprinted 2000
This edition with Study Guide 2001

All rights reserved.
No part of this publication may be reproduced or
transmitted in any form or by any means, electronic
or mechanical, including photocopy, recording, or any
information storage and retrieval system, without
permission in writing from the publisher.

Unless otherwise indicated, biblical quotations are from
the New International Version © 1973, 1978, 1984
by the International Bible Society.

Verses marked AV are from the Authorized Version
(crown copyright).

ISBN 0 85476 859 9

Published by
KINGSWAY PUBLICATIONS
Lottbridge Drove, Eastbourne, BN23 6NT, England.
Email: books@kingsway.co.uk

Designed and produced for the publishers by
Bookprint Creative Services, P.O. Box 827, BN21 3YJ, England.
Printed in Great Britain.

contents

acknowledgements

I would like to thank Alisdair Semple, the senior pastor at Reigate & Redhill Community Church, without whom this project would never have got off the ground. When I was approached out of the blue by the publisher to write a book, I was rather surprised! Alisdair encouraged me to say 'yes', which proved decisive. I would also like to thank everyone at Reigate & Redhill Community Church for their tremendous support.

I am indebted to my wife Julia in more ways than anyone reading this book could imagine. In particular, she read the manuscript and provided numerous helpful comments, cleverly feeding a newborn baby in the process!

This book was born out of a visit to the Brownsville Assembly of God Church in Pensacola, Florida, where for the first time I found myself in a 'revival'. Like many around the world, I am so grateful for the faithful prayer and witness that God has established there.

Where I have unknowingly repeated the words of other writers and preachers, I apologize.

I might be expected to dedicate this book to everyone who longs for a revival of biblical Christianity to sweep the United Kingdom, and for the church to be restored to a New Testament pattern. But this book is actually dedicated to anyone reading this who doesn't know what I'm talking about.

preface

The first time I opened the Bible to read it for myself, I promise you I heard a little voice say, 'You've just become the saddest teenager in Britain! Who reads the Bible? Get a life.' I was 16 years old.

If you're more likely to fly to the moon than read the Bible then this book is for you.

You're about to read a dramatized summary of what the Bible says will happen to you when you die. In each chapter, I've made up a story around ten points which appear in **bold type**. Most of the information in bold type is agreed by Christians everywhere to be the plain basic teaching of the Bible.

Be warned though – this book is an attempt to get you to read the Bible for yourself. And you'll notice, where the Bible is quoted directly, that a reference is given in a footnote. This consists of the name of the original 'book' in the Bible (which you'll find listed on the Contents page at the front of the Bible), followed by the chapter number in that book, followed by the verse number in that chapter. So 'Hebrews 9:27' means 'the book of Hebrews, chapter 9, verse 27.

I hope you find reading this book a rewarding experience – one way or another, you are in it.

Adrian Holloway

1

horrified – the non-christian

How can they believe in the one of whom they have not heard?
And how can they hear without someone preaching to them?
(Romans 10:14)

'For heaven's sake, Daniel, come on, we're not going to be late!' That's how my mum woke me up on 10th July 2000. Weird to think how normal a day it was. Mum was giving me a lift to college and I was always late getting up. It's the mind-numbing predictability of it all that still gets me. I've since thought that Mum probably said exactly the same thing the previous year at exactly the same time in the morning. You'd think the day you die would have some sort of spooky build-up with spooky music, but I got dressed watching *The Big Breakfast*.

Seventeen years old, doing English, History and Media Studies A levels. Perhaps someone at the local paper is writing up the story right now. I bet they'll publish an old school photo of me which I really hate. I've got bad hair in it, a wonky tie, and look like low-life scum. The stark caption underneath will read 'Daniel (17):' with the inevitable adjective 'tragic'. I hope someone at my funeral says my ambition was to be a writer. Anyway, I'll settle for a mention on the early evening news.

How did I die? In the back of the car, sitting next to my sister who was reading a *Simpsons* book, while I half-listened to some sad local radio phone-in my mum wanted on. Ten minutes into the journey – sometime after 8.30 in the morning – I was dead. We were hit by a lorry on a dual carriageway. I can draw you a map if you like.

The next thing I knew – I'm not exaggerating – the next thing I knew I was on this sort of conveyer belt hurtling forward. It was really quick. And I got a buzz out of it – even though I was dead! This was a revelation in itself! Anyway, it felt like I was back playing *Grand Theft Auto* on PlayStation the night before, except that instead of thrashing through an urban jungle, I was on a hospital trolley steaming down a corridor, slamming through swing doors. I wasn't in any pain at this point, by the way.

Here's the freaky bit – I don't know whether that was me in the hospital or not. All I know is that the next thing I was conscious of was standing in a bright yellow room! This was really real. I had my normal body with no injuries, the clothes I was wearing in the car when we crashed – and there before me was … him!

I don't know why I feel so embarrassed to describe him. He looked cool. He was at least seven feet tall, suntanned and dressed in a single white robe. It sounds a bit gay but he looked really impressive. He wasn't really smiling, but I sensed he was a smiley person. I could imagine him in real life as a ... sort of kind headmaster. But was this real life?

He told me to stand up.

'Daniel,' he said.

For the first time in my life, in death in fact, I felt like I was in a film. I also wanted to laugh. 'You know my name?'

'Daniel ...'

'Is all this real?' I interrupted. 'It seems real. Where am I? Who are you?' At this point I was ready for anything. I half-expected him to say he was from the planet Krypton. On the other hand, I was also rifling through *X-Files* episodes in my mind.

'Daniel, I want you to listen carefully to me. What I am about to say to you is the truth. You are dead and you're going to experience what happens when you die, just like everyone else.'

I slumped down cross-legged on the floor. He sounded very serious. I was struggling. I asked, 'Is it good? I mean, will I be OK?'

Silence.

Then I asked, 'Am I going to go back as something – be ... what's it called, reincarnated?'

'Follow me, Daniel,' the angel replied, as if auditioning for a take-me-to-your-leader bit part in the original *Star Trek*.

'You are going to see many things. What you don't understand, I will explain to you. We must go.'

It was almost comical, apart from the fact that I felt totally out of my depth and scared. 'And who are you?'

'I am an angel, Daniel.'

'F*** Me!'

A flash of anger came over the angel's face. I'd never felt guilty about swearing until that moment. But the whole reality of it all was beginning to kick in, and I was half-pleased to have met an angel and half-terrified about the fact that I felt totally unprepared for whatever was going to happen next. My stomach suddenly began churning and almost immediately I vomited in the corner. I was now really scared.

The angel got up and opened a door. A wall of noise from outside hit us. There were loads of people right in the doorway, talking to each other, shouting, laughing, some even dancing round in a circle like Morris Dancers – except, they didn't wave hankies and they were Indian-looking.

Safety in numbers, I thought. This cheered me up slightly. Leaving my diced carrots on the floor, I got up and, feeling very groggy and embarrassed, followed the angel out of the room.

Then we saw a panoramic view that took my breath away! As far as the eye could see there was what I can only describe as a human snake. What was I supposed to make of this? 'So now I'm with the entire human race, or so it looks?' I blurted out.

'These people are queuing up, waiting to be judged,' the angel said, as I looked down the line at thousands of people.

Now it began to hit me. This is what happens to people

when they die! It's something I'd never really thought about. Come to think of it, I don't even know that I'd ever so much as talked to anyone about it.

'This must be religious?' I asked the angel.

'What do you mean?' he replied.

'I mean, is all this religious or is it real?'

'These people are real, and God is going to judge them, so I suppose you'd say …'

'Religion is real.' I finished his sentence. Which I don't think I normally did, but I felt nervous. I felt nervous because looking at these people queuing up was making me nervous.

'Daniel, there's so much to say about all this. **I'm going to try and summarize things under ten headings for you, so listen up. The first thing, which I hope you've understood already, is that God is real.'**

(Internally I registered the first really positive feeling I'd had since getting into the car that morning, which still seemed only a few minutes before. You see I am pretty sure I believed in God. I thought to myself that this could only do me good.)

'And the second is that we are all accountable to him.'

'What does that mean?'

'These people are about to find out, and so are you!'

As we looked at the queue close up, I began searching for a familiar face. I didn't recognize anyone. I can't think why I found that strange.

After some hours going along the queue (or was it minutes, I'm not sure what the deal was with time), I heard English spoken for the first time. Four men all laughed out loud at the same time as if one of them had just told the punchline of a joke. And get this! ... They were talking about Premiership football! I felt quite at home! They didn't seem too bothered about this 'accountable' business.

'They think God's just like them,' the angel said. 'These are some of the God-will-forgive-me-that's-his-job brigade. They half-expect to find God reading *Esquire* magazine, and cracking open the lagers.' It bugged me that the angel seemed totally tuned in. What did God know about me? It didn't bear thinking about, so I tried not to.

After some time walking up by the side of the queue, we reached the front. People were stepping forward one at a time onto a white escalator.

Then it was our turn.

'Daniel, look at me for a second,' the angel said. 'Daniel, the Bible describes the scene you are about to see. A man called John saw a vision of it and wrote it down. It's in one of the books of the Bible, Revelation.'

I'd heard of Revelation, 666 and the number of the beast. Again, I hoped this might score me some points in the scheme of things. But what was the scheme of things?

The angel produced a black, leather Bible from a box that he picked up. As he began to read, we were rising up through shining whiteness. There was a sort of stadium in the distance.

As we got closer, it looked more like a theatre or a posh courtroom with a brilliant light at its centre.

The angel read from his Bible:

Then I saw a great white throne and him who was seated on it. Earth and sky fled from his presence, and there was no place for them. And I saw the dead, great and small, standing before the throne, and books were opened. Another book was opened, which is the book of life. The dead were judged according to what they had done as recorded in the books. The sea gave up the dead that were in it, and death and Hades gave up the dead that were in them, and each person was judged according to what he had done. Then death and Hades were thrown into the lake of fire. The lake of fire is the second death. If anyone's name was not found written in the book of life, he was thrown into the lake of fire.[1]

I can't regurgitate my reaction to this very clearly, because I simply lost control of myself. I do remember shouting. I think I also started hitting myself. Anyway, just at the moment he finished reading about 'the lake of fire', while I was screaming 'F*** No!' or something similar, we arrived at the upper perimeter of the courtroom.

And I thought dying in a car crash was the shock of my life! Right now, I felt like the insides had been ripped out of me. My name wasn't going to be in the 'book of life' – I'd never even heard of it!

'This is it, the final judgement', the angel said.

---

1. Revelation 20:11–15.

I was just shouting, 'No, please, no' again and again at the angel as a shuddering noise went through me. I was shaken like a rag doll and then ...

There before me was the most amazing sight I had ever seen. A blast of brightness hit us, as if we'd suddenly been brought face to face with the sun. I wanted to melt, but I remained conscious and could still see.

Here's the stunning thing about it all – the source of this light was a person! A young man, seated on a white throne on a raised platform. There was a surging power about him. The very atmosphere around him throbbed like a rocket on a launch pad. There were other ... er ... beings behind him to either side. I could see that books were lying open, just as the angel – I mean the Bible – had said. I wondered again about this 'book of life'.

I looked at the young man and then turned face down on the ground. I asked, 'Who is he?'

'The man on the throne is God's Son, Jesus Christ, who has been given authority to judge by his Father. This too is explained in the Bible.'[1]

'But how many people realize this?'

The angel replied, 'God has assured everyone that this is the case by raising Christ from the dead. The Bible says that God *has set a day when he will judge the world with justice by the man he has appointed, and he has given proof of this to all men by raising him from the dead.*'[2]

---

1. John 5:27; Acts 10:42; 2 Timothy 4:1.
2. Acts 17:31.

'I don't know what you're talking about … I don't know the Bible … Look …' I hauled myself up to about the angel's chest-level. 'Does everyone get judged? Even people like me who aren't religious and don't know anything about the Bible?'

'Yes,' the angel said. 'Look, I said I would summarize everything in ten points. **Well this is a third point: There is a final judgement for all – no matter who you are or what you believe.** We are now at the end of all time. The earth as you knew it has been … er … sort of recycled and upgraded. Everyone who ever lived on it is being judged here. **A fourth point is that Jesus Christ is the judge at this final judgement. Fifth: everyone is judged by their deeds as recorded in books.**

'Come on,' the angel said, suddenly animated, pointing to the centre of the courtroom, 'I particularly want you to see what's about to happen. Let's watch Christ judging these people. Christ himself described what we're about to see when he was on the old earth. Listen carefully.'

In front of the judge, who I now recognized as being Jesus Christ, were a small group of people. They seemed so puny and weak and yet, with great boldness, they spoke to Christ on the white throne as if they had been his friends. They said, *'Lord, Lord, did we not prophesy in your name, and in your name drive out demons and perform many miracles?'*

And then he replied, *'I never knew you. Away from me, you evildoers!'* [1]

They were stunned. I was too. They stood there speechless,

---

1. Matthew 7:22–23.

horrified – just staring. And with a sweep of his arm he sent them away.

'But these people were religious!' I protested.

'Yes they were,' the angel replied.

'Doesn't that count for anything?' I asked.

'Daniel, what did I read you from Revelation? Remember? All of their deeds are recorded in books. Just think about that for a moment. Everything you have ever done, Daniel, is recorded in those books.' He pointed at the books as if I wasn't worried enough by the sight of them. 'Besides, these people, Daniel, may have been prophets, but Jesus said they were false prophets.'[1]

I said nothing. It was the first time I'd shut up. I immediately thought about Sarah Calder. She was the girl I'd lost my virginity with. I felt so guilty about it because all the kids at school said I'd hurt her. I was sort of blacklisted for a whole term because of it. Here I was, dead, thinking about Sarah Calder!

'Just things we've done?' I asked, desperately hoping for some reassurance but expecting none.

'No. Christ said, *I tell you that men will have to give account on the day of judgment for every careless word they have spoken.*'[2]

'But I can never remember all that!'

'No, but God can, and it's all written down in the books.'

Those books again.

---

1. Matthew 7:15.
2. Matthew 12:36.

'Is there anything that he will overlook,' I asked, 'sort of pass over?'

'No,' the angel replied, '*God will judge men's secrets.*[1] Christ said, *There is nothing hidden that will not be disclosed.*[2] In fact, Christ said that words you have whispered will be *proclaimed from the roofs.*[3] **My sixth point is that everything you've done, thought or said is recorded in the books, and everyone has sinned and fallen short of God's perfect standard.**'[4]

'And everyone's going to know what I've done?'

'Exactly.'

'This is a total disaster! Is there any good news?'

'Yes, I mean, from your point of view, the fact that every judgement God makes is entirely fair is good news.'[5]

A pause.

'Look for a moment at Christ on the white throne.'

As I did, I felt a sense of awe; in fact I bowed down on my knees as I looked at him.

'How could a being as pure as he is allow your wrongdoing into heaven?'

This was a piercing question. It was also the first mention of heaven, and the thought of it seemed so sweet, but I actually found myself totally in agreement with the angel. There was no way that someone like me could dwell with

---

1. Romans 2:16.
2. Luke 8:17.
3. Luke 12:3.
4. Romans 3:23.
5. Genesis 18:25; Deuteronomy 32:4; Psalm 9:8; Romans 2:11.

such a perfect being as the man seated on that throne.

I was still downhearted, but as I looked at Christ, any sense of being aggrieved left me. Here was my Creator. I pictured myself, unborn, miniature, in the womb. How helpless and totally dependent I was then and am now. In between were 17 years of me fancying myself. All my life, every breath – it was all provided by this awesome Creator who was now going to hold me to account for it. For a second, I managed to put my feelings in one compartment of my brain and the rest of me in another. My conclusion? This was common sense!

After all, had I lived for God? ... No.

Had I sought him? ... No.

Had I even thanked him for giving me life? ... No. I had just grabbed my chance to enjoy myself and got on with the serious business of doing what I wanted to do. With these thoughts in my mind, I looked back at Christ on the white throne. There was no injustice here. However I was still not facing up to the full reality of my own fate. *'I never knew you. Away from me.'* [1] was surely what he'd say to me.

Somehow, though, I clung to a crumb of comfort, and this was it ... I was a spectator at this judgement – I hadn't joined the queue yet!

From our vantage point just above the back row of the courtroom, we had so far seen numerous people come and go. Everyone had been sent away by Christ with chilling words. They each departed in some agony or distress. I shuddered to

---

1. Matthew 7:23.

think of it … 'The lake of fire?'

I don't know how many people we saw judged. Perhaps it was about three hundred while we were watching. One by one they came in. The things they said to Christ became predictable. These people had genuinely believed they were good enough to go to heaven. And I could hear my voice echoing each appeal they made to the throne. And every time Christ's final reply was the same.

'But I spent twelve years looking after my disabled mother,' was a heart-wrenching one from a black lady.

'I never knew you. Away from me.' [1]

Another woman in tears said: 'I always put the children first.'

'I never knew you. Away from me.'

'I've done the best I could.'

'I never knew you. Away from me.'

'I never killed anyone.'

'I never knew you. Away from me.'

After hearing Christ's reply, one Spanish- or Italian-looking man was about to say something like 'Come off it!' Then he stopped himself. His reaction had been instinctive, impulsive. He checked himself and looked at the throne. I did too – pure and white. Christ wasn't a referee you could shout and swear at. This was no Sunday morning park kick about. Our Spanish friend crumbled in awe. He fell on his knees, not in pleading, but in regret. It was too late to change anything.

---

1. Matthew 7:23.

I could picture him on Waterloo station having just run for the last train home only to see it pulling away without him.

Others craned their necks trying to see what was in the books. What a leveller this judgement was! Some of them were rich I suppose, but the rich were treated just the same as tramps. I felt some sort of satisfaction in the marvellous equality of it all. Power and influence counted for nothing here, and all were treated alike. But where were these people going next? Where were my family and friends headed? The 'lake of fire'?

Just as I was trying to imagine it, there was an eruption of noise. Everyone was on their feet and trumpets sounded.

'What's going on now?' I asked the angel.

'A wonderful triumph, Daniel. This young girl's name has been found written in the book of life.'

'What?' I stared at her. She was Asian, and her face shone. She reminded me of a kid in GCSE Geography.

Then Christ said to her, *'Come, you who are blessed by my Father; take your inheritance, the kingdom prepared for you since the creation of the world.'* [1]

'He hasn't said that to anyone else yet, has he?'

'This is the first one since you've been watching, Daniel. **What you are seeing here illustrates my seventh point. Everyone deserves the punishment of death because everyone has sinned against God, but those whose names are found in the book of life will escape death. In fact, they go to heaven!'**

---

1. Matthew 25:34.

'What? How come?'

'OK – I need to explain point seven. For now, just consider that this young woman knew Christ would say this to her because she'd read it in the Bible!'

The angel was already turning to the page – I was spellbound.

'Daniel let me read part of this to you because it describes what you are seeing. Christ called himself the Son of man, and he said, *When the Son of Man comes in his glory, and all the angels with him, he will sit on his throne in heavenly glory. All the nations will be gathered before him, and he will separate the people one from another as a shepherd separates the sheep from the goats. He will put the sheep on his right and the goats on his left. Then the King will say to those on his right, "Come, you who are blessed by my Father; take your inheritance, the kingdom prepared for you since the creation of the world."* '[1]

'So what has this girl done that gets her accepted?'

'Nothing.'

'Nothing?!'

'This girl hasn't done anything to make herself acceptable to God.'

'Then why is she accepted?' I asked more out of envy than curiosity.

'She has been accepted because someone else took the punishment she should have got. Somebody who was perfect volunteered to be punished in her place. He took her sin. She

---

1. Matthew 25:31–34.

his perfection. They swapped!'

'But that's outrageous! How can that be fair?'

What I said seemed to remind the angel of something pleasing to him. He laughed and said, 'You wouldn't expect it, would you! But that's the beauty of what God's done! The fact is that this girl did nothing to make herself acceptable to God, yet as you can see she has been declared righteous by Christ. She walks free from the courtroom into heaven.'

'But surely she must have been more religious than the other lot who got sent away, the ones who did the driving out of the demons and the prophesying?' (Which I thought sounded cool – fun even!) 'This cannot be right,' I said to the angel, feeling quite indignant.

'Oh really, and who are you to say what can and cannot be right?' the angel put me in my place. He continued, 'Daniel, to understand why this girl is being accepted by God, I must ask you what you know about Jesus Christ.'

'Well, I know how there was no room at the inn and all that. He was Jewish. The Son of God, crucified for the sins of the world.'

'Let me stop you there. Where did you get that from?'

'I don't know. Maybe school assemblies.'

'What does "He was crucified for the sins of the world" mean?'

'I don't know exactly.'

'Well, you know that Christ was executed by being nailed to a wooden cross?'

'Of course ...'

'Christ is unique. He never sinned. He was perfect. When he died, he took the punishment you should have got for everything you have ever done wrong. And he was punished for the sins of everyone else, including this girl's.'

'You mean we're looking at the same Jesus who was on the cross?' I was awestruck. 'But he looks so fantastic!'

'Well, he's risen from the dead and ascended to his Father's side, and his Father has given him authority to judge. But even as he judges this girl, he knows that he took all her sin when he was crucified on the cross.

'Let me explain it to you again by telling you a story,' the angel continued. 'Imagine you're in Florida in the year 2000 and you walk into a shopping mall and shoot someone dead.'

'But I'd never do that!' I objected.

'I know,' the angel replied, 'but I need to make up a story which will show you that sin leads to the punishment of death, and in Florida, as you probably remember, you were liable to get the electric chair for murder.'

'OK,' I said.

The angel continued, 'So you shoot someone dead and immediately you're arrested. You wait for your trial to come round. At the trial, a security camera videotape is produced on which you are clearly identifiable as the killer.'

'Like on *Crimewatch*?'

'Yes, OK, like on *Crimewatch*. Anyway, the evidence is stacked against you, and the judge is about to sentence you to death when a stranger bursts into the courtroom.

'He pushes past the security guards and makes his way

towards you standing in the dock. And to the amazement of the press reporters and your family in the gallery, the judge allows the disturbance to continue. Then the stranger pushes you out of the dock and stands there in your place.

'The judge does nothing to stop the stranger. Instead he looks straight at him and says, "I sentence you to death!" The whole courtroom gasps. The judge bangs his hammer on the desk. The trial is over and you're left standing on the courtroom floor, free! The police handcuff the stranger and begin to lead him away to death row!

'As the stranger passes, you ask him, "Why did you do that?" and he replies: "Because I love you." Somehow that doesn't seem enough of an explanation. You wander out into the foyer of the courthouse. Then you overhear the press talking. The stranger has been recognized after all. He is the judge's only son! Now you are in awe of the judge. Then the judge pushes past the reporters. You ask him, "Your honour, please, why have you done this for me?" and he answers, "Because I love you!"'

For once the angel didn't have to explain any further. I understood instantly why this Christ was so impressive, why he received such worship and praise from the Asian girl. He had loved her so much that he had given up his own life for her, just like the stranger in the courtroom. The penny dropped. Christ had died as a kind of substitute for her. God, the judge, sacrificed his Son.

But this girl must have accepted this news during her life on earth, whereas if I'd ever heard it, so that I understood it,

I knew I wouldn't have been the slightest bit interested. I wasn't the religious type and was perfectly happy as I was.

'So somebody told her about God sending his own Son to death? Or did she read it in the Bible?'

'Both!' replied the angel. 'And she believed it. But she died from meningitis two weeks later. Yet Christ says in the Bible that *Whoever believes in him is not condemned, but whoever does not believe stands condemned already because he has not believed in the name of God's one and only Son.*[1]

'Daniel, I think you're now ready for me **to explain my seventh point.**'

'Let me have a crack at it,' I said, hoping that spitting the words out would make me feel better. 'Jesus is that Judge's Son. Jesus is a perfect substitute. He swapped his perfection for this girl's sin. He died in her place, so she escapes punishment and goes to heaven. Is that right?'

The angel said, '**Yes. The punishment for sin is death. But God loves people so much, he sent his Son Jesus Christ to die in their place. Anyone who truly follows Christ therefore avoids the punishment of death and receives forgiveness. In fact they are considered as blameless as Christ himself. These are the people whose names appear in the book of life. They go to heaven.**'

'So why didn't somebody get hold of me and drum it into me so that I could have believed?'

'I don't know, Daniel.'

---

1. John 3:18.

'OK then, please tell me, in that Bible passage you were reading, does it say that Christ sends people away just like we've been seeing up here?'

'Oh yes,' the angel looked at the passage again. 'Christ says to those on his left, *Depart from me, you who are cursed, into the eternal fire prepared for the devil and his angels.*' [1]

This was the first time the devil had been mentioned. I hadn't been surprised to find out that God exists, though I'd done absolutely nothing about it while on earth. But I was surprised to find out that the devil was real. He was nowhere to be seen here, though.

Now, as you're reading this, you might wonder how I can carry on when my own fate is looking so bleak. The truth is that I was so taken with the wonder of looking at Christ, that every time I looked at him I thought about him rather than me, but when I looked away, I realized how totally unworthy of him I was. Still the Asian girl who got to heaven fascinated me.

'So is she the only one?'

'Oh no,' the angel said. 'Look around you.'

All around us were other people; they had somehow blended into the scene, and seeing as I had been staring at Christ most of the time, I wasn't surprised I hadn't noticed them more.

'**Here's the eighth point in my summary: Christians help in the work of judgement.**' [2]

---

1. Matthew 25:41.
2. 1 Corinthians 6:2–3; Revelation 20:4.

By this stage, my head was spinning. I decided I'd been dead for too long already! What really blew me away was the fact that there were people for whom none of the eight points I'd encountered so far would come as a surprise! They knew about every one of them! Like seeing the exam paper the night before, they knew all the questions and the answers before death. No shocks for them! Who were these people? Why didn't they tell us more about what they knew to be true? I was getting angry just thinking about it.

I was trying to dredge up from my memory a conversation I'd once had with a girl at college called Becky Mason (the only proper Christian I think I'd known), when the angel started to stare at me. 'Daniel, it's time for me to show you what has happened to those who have been sent away to eternal punishment.'

This was what I had been dreading more than anything else. For the first time I was shaking, and the angel had to carry me – which he seemed to do effortlessly. We had been looking head-on at Christ from the rear of the courtroom – now we walked to his left, to the place where everyone except the Asian girl had been dragged.

As we reached this area, the crowd erupted again behind us. Another name had been found in the book of life! I spun round. With all my heart I wanted it to be Becky Mason, because I wanted to give her a piece of my mind. 'Oi, Becky!' I would have said. 'Why didn't you tell me? Why didn't you warn me! What was the problem? Wasn't it important enough? Only a matter of life and death, Becky!' Of course it wasn't her. Instead it was an elderly Japanese- or Chinese-looking man.

He was going to be in heaven for ever. I still shuddered to think that so many hadn't made it. Surely whatever hell was, I was going to experience it, when my turn came to reach the front of the queue and appear before Christ.

What now? The angel began to say something more, 'I have two things left to explain to you in my summary.' I wanted to interrupt and ask if he'd ever heard of Becky Mason, but I hadn't got the guts. He continued, **'Point nine is that hell is a real place and real people go there.** I'll explain the tenth point when we are inside.'

'Stop,' I said, having had more than enough shocks. 'Please, tell me what the Bible says about hell first before I see anything. I don't think I can take any more!'

'Very well,' the angel replied. 'The Bible says that God *will punish those who do not know God and do not obey the gospel of our Lord Jesus. They will be punished with everlasting destruction and shut out from the presence of the Lord and from the majesty of his power.'* [1]

Now that I had seen Christ with my own eyes, it seemed to me that being shut out from his presence was bad enough. 'Can you tell me what it's like?'

'Being in hell is an experience full of anguish and distress. Christ said repeatedly on earth that hell is a place where there will be weeping and gnashing of teeth. But you are not going

---

1. 2 Thessalonians 1:8–9.

to see everything in hell, nor will you be told its location.'

Now let me explain something to you here. Usually, no matter how bad things get in life, there's something you can think of, even the tiniest thing, that can cheer you up, even if it's just an inane thought like 'Things can only get better!' But the mind-crunching reality was that for me things would never get better – they would get worse, and then get worse still. I was on an eternal downward spiral. This was a bad trip.

'Come on,' the angel said, sensing that I was approaching a sort of hysterical despair. 'Nothing I tell you, even from the Bible, can properly prepare you for this, so let's get on with it.'

Here I blacked out, so I have no idea how close the entrance to hell is to the scene of the final judgement. This was clearly something that I wasn't going to be told. It was a bit like a documentary I saw once about hostages in Lebanon in the 1980s who got moved around with blindfolds on. The blindfold of my blackout came off as I peered into the entrance to hell. It was a cavernous hole, with masses of people swarming around it.

Another random thought – what good had football, music, clubbing or my mates done for me? Here I was in hell!

'If only I could join that Asian girl we saw.'

The angel replied, 'Christ said, *Wide is the gate and broad is the road that leads to destruction, and many enter through it. But small is the gate and narrow the road that leads to life, and only a few find it.*' [1]

---

1. Matthew 7:13–14.

I was too depressed to take it in. As we looked at the masses surrounding the entrance to hell, I knew what a slave I had been to peer pressure. Where had following the crowd led me? I now knew the in-crowd would end up in hell. I half expected to find my mates from college here already. Then I thought of them having fun on earth – or maybe they were at my funeral. What were they thinking? Was my funeral religious? I bet it was – what a joke that is! Would it sober any of them up? Probably not.

It was weird that I could think so clearly despite my overwrought emotions and the horror of what I saw as the angel led me closer to the entrance to hell. As we neared it, skirting around the edge of the crowds, we could see that immediately beneath those at the front of the crowd was … a lake of fire! Like water thundering over Niagara Falls, the crowds were crashing down onto the lake. It was awful.

The people in the lake below reminded me of the *Titanic* film, at the end with all those souls shrieking in the water. My sister must have watched that film twenty times, but the consolation for me when I watched it, was that some of the passengers survived. But could some of the real Titanic survivors have ended up in this lake of fire? The sickening irony of it all! Imagine being saved from the world's most famous disaster, then another so many years of useless living without God on earth, and then hell for ever after dying peacefully in your sleep!

And they're called survivors!

The angel again opened his Bible and said, 'Listen to how

Christ finishes the parable of the weeds: *As the weeds are pulled up and burned in the fire, so it will be at the end of the age. The Son of Man will send out his angels, and they will weed out of his kingdom everything that causes sin and all who do evil. They will throw them into the fiery furnace, where there will be weeping and gnashing of teeth. Then the righteous will shine like the sun in the kingdom of their Father. He who has ears, let him hear.*[1]

As I looked at these people writhing in agony in the lake, it reminded me of gory moments from videos my friends and I had dared each other to nick from the corner shop when we were 12. I think we'd only succeeded once or twice. But there was a startling difference. Gruesome scenes in those films resulted in death – full stop. ... This was torture, so it seemed, without end.

'What does the Bible say about how long they're punished for?'

'I've already told you,' the angel shouted back, trying to make himself heard above the groanings of those in the lake. 'Do you remember the end of the parable of the sheep and the goats? Christ says that *they will go away to eternal punishment, but the righteous to eternal life.*'[2]

'I don't get it,' I answered, staring blankly.

'It's the same word.'

'What is?'

---

1. Matthew 13:40–43.
2. Matthew 25:46.

'The Bible uses the same word "eternal" to describe the punishment and the life. Daniel, these people will suffer in hell for just as long as the Christians will be in heaven – for ever! Elsewhere in the Bible, Christ says that this fire *never goes out.*' [1]

While humans were being shoved down onto the lake, we walked around the perimeter. There was a terrible smell, by the way; in fact there's so much stinky grizzly stuff I haven't mentioned. Anyway, the angel began pointing to a particular man who was floundering in the lake and shouting.

'Look at this one. This guy is mentioned in the Bible,' he said.

The angel continued, 'On earth he was rich. He was dressed in fine clothes and he lived in luxury every day. Outside his house lay a beggar called Lazarus. Lazarus was covered with sores. Even dogs would come and lick his sores. Anyway, Lazarus longed to be able to eat even the crumbs that fell from the rich man's table.

'Well both these men died. The rich man expected to go to heaven, but he's ended up here, being tormented in hell. Meanwhile Lazarus has gone to heaven.'

I looked at the rich man. Despite the generations between us, I could identify with him. Neither of us thought we'd ever be here. Then the rich man suddenly shouted out, *'Father Abraham, have pity on me and send Lazarus to dip the tip of his finger in water and cool my tongue, because I am in agony in this fire.'* [2]

---

1. Mark 9:43.
2. Luke 16:24.

'Did you hear that?' the angel said. 'It's as if it's being acted out before us just as Jesus described.'

'Who's Abraham?' I asked the angel.

'It's a long story, but the bottom line is that Abraham is someone in heaven who this rich man wants a favour from. Anyway, Jesus tells us that Abraham replied at this point, *Son, remember that in your lifetime you received your good things, while Lazarus received bad things, but now he is comforted here and you are in agony. And besides all this, between us and you a great chasm has been fixed, so that those who want to go from here to you cannot, nor can anyone cross over from there to us.*'[1]

Then the rich man again cried out to heaven, right on cue, *'Then I beg you, father, send Lazarus to my father's house, for I have five brothers. Let him warn them, so that they will not also come to this place of torment.'*[2]

I turned to the angel, who read me Abraham's reply: *'They have Moses and the Prophets; let them listen to them.'*[3]

'Moses!' I interrupted. 'Moses, as in *The Prince of Egypt*?'

'Yes,' the angel replied.

'What has Moses got to do with this?'

'Well, he wrote the bit of the Bible this man could have read.'

At this point, I was shocked by what the rich man said next. *'No, father Abraham ... but if someone from the dead goes to them, they will repent.'*[4]

---

1. Luke 16:25–26.
2. Luke 16:27–28.
3. Luke 16:29.
4. Luke 16:30.

This man was still saying no to heaven, even when he was himself in hell! The fact that he had ended up in hell, clearly hadn't sobered him up one bit. Here he was in hell, shouting the odds at heaven, and trying to boss Abraham around, whoever he is!

In that instant, as I watched the rich man saying 'no', it struck me that this too was a sin, and maybe part of the reason why these people were being punished for ever. Were they constantly committing fresh sins that required fresh punishment?

I was appalled by the arrogance of this man. To be honest, I'd never really thought about how our selfishness and arrogance affected God. But the other side of the grave these sins repulsed me.

The angel continued: 'Abraham replied, *If they do not listen to Moses and the Prophets, they will not be convinced even if someone rises from the dead.*' [1]

A miracle like someone rising from the dead would certainly have got my attention, but this reply left me reeling. The Bible has more clout than an outstanding miracle! But I never knew that until now, and now it was too late!

At various points, like this one for example, I was haunted by the memory of Bibles lined up on the shelf in the RE room at school. I cannot recall ever having any enthusiasm for opening one of them. Yet if I had, I could have read the story of the rich man and Lazarus at school. Now my mind was racing! If I had read it, would I have believed? If I had read

---

1. Luke 16:31.

Christ describing this conversation between the rich man and Lazarus, would it have swayed me?

Suddenly, a flashback to my childhood. I remembered sitting on top of the stairs listening in on a shocking conversation between my parents. They were swearing at each other in a way I'd never heard them do before. (A year later they separated and they're now divorced.) Listening to them fight was like suddenly tuning in to the truth! By accident, I'd discovered what my mum and dad really thought about each other.

I could have tuned in to the truth in RE simply by reading about the rich man's fate!

It was all so frustrating. This must be where the gnashing of teeth comes in. So near and yet so far! I thought of Mr Grant, my RE teacher. He was always telling us how the Bible was like – what's it called – Chinese whispers. He was happy to tell us he didn't believe much of it.

Well, Mr Grant, I'm feeling the heat right now in one of the bits you don't believe in! Grant was more enthusiastic, so it seemed, about other religions, but he failed to make any of them sound interesting to any of us. What relevance did all his God talk have to do with our lives? Some kids in our class would bunk off RE. (Mr Grant was very laid back.)

So near to the truth in that room – those Bibles just sitting there – and yet so far! I felt angry with Mr Grant. Why hadn't they appointed a teacher who could have made it interesting to us? The truth about Christ was attractive enough. I decided that God had a serious PR problem on earth, or in Britain anyway.

The angel then said, 'It only remains for me to tell you **the tenth and final point of my summary. God is holy and just and he must punish sin. All sin is punished either on the cross of Christ or in hell. Hell is the punishment every sinner deserves, but because Christ was punished on the cross, his followers escape hell. Those who go to hell suffer different degrees of punishment there.** Christ said it would be more bearable for some people than others [1] and that some would suffer more than others. [2]

'So how much does it hurt for those who suffer most?'

The angel replied: 'Daniel, how much it hurts physically is not the big deal. You've only seen the outward suffering of those in hell, but it's the inward, emotional suffering you haven't seen that's the worst of it. You've only seen symbols or pictures of what's going on inside these people. The fire is like the burning frustration these people feel. That's why they gnash their teeth. Please don't think that it's because hell's so hot that people writhe in agony – it's the regret and anger they feel that makes it so unbearable for them.'

The angel paused. Something was up. He turned back to me. 'Daniel, I cannot show you any more of hell; we cannot go any further. You yourself have not yet been judged, and that is what must happen now. It's time for us to go back to the queue of those awaiting judgement. But this time, Daniel, you must join the queue yourself.'

---

1. Matthew 10:15; 11:22–24.
2. Luke 12:47–48.

As we left hell, my first thought was that I wished I had never been born. It was startling to think how pleasurable non-existence seemed at that moment. I now knew that there is a fate worse than death, and its name is hell. If only my parents had never conceived me!

Then I thought of the Asian girl. Her faith seemed so sensible and heroic as she stood before Christ. I could picture his expression, looking into her eyes, saying *Come*. Now I realized my greatest wish was not non-existence; it was to hear Christ say to me, *Come*. But it was too late!

The angel was carrying me again, and I could hardly focus as he walked with me in his arms back down the queue. At that moment, even in my weakness, I realized I had the chance to do something pleasing to God before I was consigned to hell. Summoning what little energy I had, I jumped up out of the angel's hands and stumbled towards people in the queue.

I was in luck, there were people speaking English nearby.

'You need to be a Christian or you'll go to hell!' I screamed with all the strength I could muster.

They completely ignored me, thinking I was some sort of maniac.

Another flashback. This time I remembered being in my bedroom at home, reading the lyrics of a Manic Street Preachers CD.

Now I was a manic street preacher, not outside Boots on a Saturday morning yelling at passing shoppers, but at the queue for the last judgement! The CD was called *This is my truth, tell me yours*. Could God have supernaturally made me think this?

I screamed out, 'It doesn't matter what you think the truth is – there is a whopping great judgement up there and if you're not a Christian, you'll be punished in hell for ever for your sins.'

I realized that I hadn't explained what I meant by a Christian. After all, I suppose I would have described myself as a Christian while I was on earth. I was new to this preaching business, and it struck me that what I had said wouldn't have helped anyone who considered themselves to be a Christian but actually wasn't. I was just about to answer the question 'What is a Christian?' when I realized that no one had asked it. No one was paying attention.

I staggered down the queue another hundred yards. Again I found some English speakers, but this time, rather than shouting at them, I listened to their conversation.

They were talking nonsense.

'I was baptized as a baby,' one said.

'Yeah, you went to church,' said another, 'but you only went three times: for your christening, wedding and funeral, and that means that two out of three times you were carried in!'

There was more laughter. These people were totally unconcerned about their fate.

'Hey, listen!'

Again, no response.

'It's no use,' the angel said. He had been standing behind me all the time! 'They can't hear you.'

I was upset by this. 'But think about what I've got to say. Why doesn't God let them hear me now? I could do something for him by warning these people!'

'Once you're dead it's too late! There's no second chance here,' the angel said. 'The Bible says, *Man is destined to die once, and after that to face judgment.*' [1]

It dawned on me that none of the people I'd preached at had heard a word I'd said. There was no preaching between death and judgement because at death it was too late!

'We saw people in hell who'd had chances to believe,' the angel reminded me. 'Many of these in the queue had every opportunity to believe, but they would not.'

You'd imagine people queuing up for judgement would be like jelly, quivering in fear, but the truth is that some of the people I heard were talking as if God owed them a favour.

As I spoke to the angel about the presumption these people displayed, he told me something that made sense of so much I had seen on earth. The angel showed me from the Bible (the book of Romans chapter 1 and verse 24) that judgement starts before death for some. It is almost as if God sees the determination of those who want to go against him and gives them over to their own desires. These people end up even more enslaved than when they began to sin in the first place.

Was I enslaved? Yes, to bad habits, to things I knew were wrong. I was horrified, by myself and by the impending judgement and subsequent punishment.

As I joined the queue, I collapsed, sobbing violently.

This wasn't like the blackout I had before our spin round hell. This was sheer emotional and physical exhaustion. I just

---

1. Hebrews 9:27.

felt under so much pressure. I don't know how often I collapsed, but I had to keep pulling myself up, until I finally reached the front of the queue.

While some around me were perking up, thinking that their troubles were at an end, I had the horrible knowledge that for those who weren't Christians their troubles were just about to begin. The only consolation was that I knew I would be in Christ's presence. I would hear his voice, even if he was going to send me away.

Finally, I reached the front of the queue. All through my life on earth I had believed that the worst thing that could happen to me was death. At this moment I felt more keenly than ever before that I had been deceived. There was something far worse than death: a punishment of torment and agony that would never end.

I looked up and saw Christ for the last time. Although I couldn't really look at him, being in his presence was terrific. I felt a mixture of admiration and fear. I knew that he would say, *'I never knew you. Away from me.'* [1] and I was thinking how fair it seemed.

Then Christ spoke: 'Daniel.' He said my name! He was departing from the script! Was he going to single me out for special punishment?

'Daniel, your time has not yet come. This is the final judgement at the end of all things and you will be judged here … but not yet. I have decided that you are to go back to

---

1. Matthew 7:23.

where you've come from. But from now on, every time you think about the cross where I died, you will understand that I love you, Dan.'

The next conscious moment, I saw my mother's face! I was alive!

Yes! Oh, yes! Thank You!

Elation!

I couldn't move or speak, so I could hardly celebrate. Of course, I was happy to see Mum too, but inside I was doing cartwheels about Jesus! What a let-off! I'd escaped hell and need never go there! I would follow Jesus, whatever happened. Then I began to think about going to heaven. It was all too much for me! Thank you, Jesus!

My body felt numb – or at least my legs did. There were tubes plugged into me, and I had no energy to do anything more than open my eyes.

As I lay there with my family around the bed, I heard my mum screaming with delight, and crying. Obviously, opening my eyes had been the first sign of life I'd shown.

☆ ☆ ☆

Here I am, six months later. I've typed everything you've just read from a wheelchair at an Internet café. My mum and sister Kate were more or less unharmed by the crash and I am now recovering fast from my injuries. The most serious were to my head, and it was these that doctors thought would be fatal. In fact they were, in a funny sort of way!

As you can imagine, as soon as I could communicate with anyone, I started to describe what happens beyond death. The biggest impact was upon my family and friends who knew I'd never been religious and they were totally at a loss to know what to make of what I said.

Perhaps you are expecting me to say that they have all become Christians, but the fact is none of them have – so far. They seem to think that I have some sort of trauma-related mental illness. I have been sent to a psychiatrist, who I am due to see for the second time next week.

Of course, I couldn't wait to go to church. I was so excited to think that I could meet people who already knew Christ. They were not likely to send me off to a psychiatrist!

So I persuaded my mother to come with me to our local church. I had cycled past it many times but never been in. There were no more than forty people there. Talk about the world's best-kept secret! We followed the service in a book. I thought the words were great and that everything we sang was spot on. Afterwards we went to the church hall for coffee. There was no one there my age, but, to my mother's embarrassment I got into conversation with a few of them, and started to describe what had happened to me. They seemed a bit shocked. Although they listened with interest, I think they were just being polite.

So that's where I'm at for the time being. I'm going again next Sunday, when I hope to talk to the minister and tell him about it. Surely, out there somewhere there must be people who will believe me.

As I sit here writing these words, there are two images I cannot get out of my mind: Christ on his white throne, and the agonies of those in hell. Christ's love and their tortured expressions stay with me every night. Can I ask you: are you going to experience Christ's love or the agonies of hell?

And if you're a Christian, here is my question to you, and don't you dodge it. Why do you keep quiet?

2

gutted – the lukewarm christian

I know your deeds, that you are neither cold nor hot. I wish you were either one or the other! So, because you are lukewarm – neither hot nor cold – I am about to spit you out of my mouth. (Revelation 3:15–16)

First of all, I've never done this before, OK? Anyway ... here we go! My name's Becky. What you're reading is what I'm saying into this little dictaphone tape recorder. They're going to tidy it up – you know, put all the commas and full stops in – when I've finished.

All I can remember is that I was walking to college with my back to the traffic. I heard a screech of brakes and then a deafening smash. I spun round to see a shower of glass and a dirty big lorry almost on top of me. It must have hit me because I blacked out and the next thing I remember is coming round, finding myself spreadeagled on the grass verge, in real pain, not being able to move my legs.

I was like this for maybe a minute, the final 60 seconds of my life as it turned out. But it was long enough to see that there were three people lying in the mangled wreckage of a car next to the lorry. A completely motionless boy, who looked about 17, and I guess his sister and their mum, both of whom were pushing him around, trying to revive him, but only getting themselves covered in his blood. It was awful.

Thinking back now to the moment before impact, I can still picture the lorry driver wide-eyed shouting at me from his cab. I couldn't hear a word. He slammed on his brakes. The lorry – what's it called? jackknifed? He couldn't avoid me and I couldn't get out of the way in time.

I'd walked this same route to school and college every day since the age of 11. It was a main road, but it wasn't exactly dangerous because there was a wide grass verge between us on the pavement and the road. Hundreds of kids walked the same way to college every day. It was about 8.30 in the morning. Then suddenly, with no warning: Game Over!

So, at the age of 18, I was dying. I felt darkness creeping over me as I sensed my body giving up. Blood was pouring from my head. It was horrible not being able to do anything about it. I could hear the drone of traffic and people screaming and footsteps running towards me. But instead of the footsteps growing louder, they grew quieter as I felt myself weakening. Then … a sudden release from the pain … silence and stillness.

Death. Complete darkness.

Then, I promise you I am not lying, it was as if someone

switched the lights back on!

Don't tell me it sounds cheesy. I am telling you that a moment later I was conscious again! Total blackness, then Ping! I still existed!

And I could feel no pain! I knew immediately my injuries had disappeared! The physical agony I felt after being thumped by the lorry had completely gone. I was alive and well! I could move my legs. But my eyes were still shut. Nervously, I opened them and ... I could see! The thrill of it! I shouted, 'Whooaa!' I was laughing. I knew what this meant: heaven!

I yelled again, and started jumping up and down. I cannot begin to describe how wonderful it was. In a split second I'd gone from my worst nightmare come true – paralysed on a grass verge knowing I was dying – to ... ultimate satisfaction. One second I was thinking, 'No! This is all wrong! I've got my whole life ahead of me; I'm going to miss out on everything.' The next, I was shouting, 'Whooaa!' in the sure knowledge that I was about to experience some serious eternal ecstasy!

Let me give you a bit of background. I need to explain that I wasn't surprised to find there was life after death. Like most of my friends at college I believed there was something more, but unlike most of my friends, my parents are total hard-core Christians. They give their lives to the church and totally believe the Bible. They brought me up to believe it too. I was baptized when I was 13, and however strange this may sound to you, I felt I knew Jesus personally. I certainly had no fear of death, although it had never occurred to me that I would die young. All the people I knew who'd died were old people.

So I wasn't surprised to find myself still alive, but I did feel relieved. To be honest, I suppose I had a nagging doubt in the back of my mind that when you're dead, you're dead. In fact, that's what my best friend at school, Anna, believes – not that we really talked about it much. I'd sometimes wondered, 'What if Anna's right?' But in the moment after death the nagging doubt was overtaken by stark reality. I opened my eyes and saw ... what?

Well, I saw a long queue of people. I couldn't see any of their faces though. They were all looking away from me, standing in a line that stretched as far as the eye could see. There was nothing else visible – everything was white. I was standing up, some distance from the end of the queue. I felt more alive and well than ever before! I started to feel my face. I wasn't a ghost or transparent. I definitely wasn't lying in a heap by a road. I started walking towards the queue, and then in a moment of sheer adrenaline, I broke into a run. I seemed to be able to run faster than ever before and running didn't use up any energy.

I may have been in the queue for hours or minutes. I can only remember talking to a couple of people. I was not really conscious of the passing of time. I just wanted to get to the front. Heaven was just moments away!

At the front of the queue, I stepped up onto what turned out to be a white escalator. I rose and rose upwards over what looked like the back of a stadium. How bizarre! As I was transported upwards, I clenched my fists in anticipation. 'In a moment, I'm going to be in heaven!'

I wondered what it would look like. Nervous but excited, the only things I could think of were pearly gates and streets of gold with St Peter at the check-in desk, and I wasn't even sure if these things were really in the Bible or whether they were just myths. Don't get me wrong, I knew heaven was going to be real. I just had no idea what to expect!

Anyway, when I came up over the back of the stadium, like a brilliant dawn on the horizon, I was engulfed in a powerful light, which burst upon me from below. I looked and looked at this light as I was lowered down and my feet touched the ground. Bright as the light was, I felt no need to squint or look away. Then as I continued to look directly into the brightness, I could tell by the outline that it was coming from a person. A normal-sized human!

I knew instinctively that this was ... Jesus! He was wearing a single white tunic and was sitting on a raised platform – a stage in fact. I was really seeing Jesus face to face! His face just glowed. The one who saved me! This was thrilling. I felt so grateful. I felt so special. I just knew he really cared about me!

It seemed like the air was on fire all around him. This was awesome! As my eyes adjusted to the light, it became clear that he was sitting on an enormous snow-white throne with a high back. He had a book, which was open on his lap. Was he going to read from it?

He looked straight at me, then down at the book. After a moment, he looked up again and smiled at me! As if he'd found my name!

This may sound arrogant, but he looked pleased to see me! He said nothing at first. He just smiled. I felt fantastic. Behind Jesus and either side of him, there were … er … people moving to and fro. I assumed these people were angels because they too had a glow about them, but nothing compared to the brightness that poured out of Jesus, who was surrounded by fire and literally lit up the place.

The angels were carrying books. In fact there were large books everywhere. Jesus then motioned to one of the angels, who produced a huge pile, which he seemed to be sorting out by checking what was written on the front covers.

Once he'd finished his task, he picked up the books, got down off the stage and started to walk towards me!

My eyes were fixed on the covers of the books as they bobbed towards me in the angel's arms. Suddenly, a flash of fear plummeted to the bottom of my stomach. I thought I could read my name on them!

With each step, the lettering on the spine of each book became clearer. Each one said my name and then the dates: '1982–2000.'

I froze. The books were placed in front of me. Then Jesus, who'd only smiled at me so far and hadn't moved, reached down onto the platform floor and with his right hand picked up a pole with a metal end on it lying beside him. The moment he grasped it, the metal end caught fire! Jesus was holding an Olympic torch! And then in one flowing movement he swung the torch up in an arc and then down onto the pile of books in front of me.

The books instantly burst into flames. I gasped and jumped backwards, feeling the heat on the shins of my legs. This was totally unexpected. Then as quickly as the fire had started, it went out! I looked down and … the books had gone! Vanished! Like the morning after a campfire, there was nothing but smouldering blackened earth and smoke!

Gazing at the charred earth, I breathed in and coughed out some smoke. I felt … gutted. A searching emptiness.

A pause.

Up to now I had been enjoying myself. This was different. What had my life amounted to? Whatever this meant, it was obviously symbolic of something about my life.

What I haven't told you yet, but what you've probably guessed by now, is that my being a 'Christian' was a bit of a joke, and it's not just me saying it – my friends said the same to my face. No way could anyone say I lived for Jesus. I believed in Christianity deep down, but it never seemed that important. I was always getting round to 'sorting myself out'.

But if only … if only I'd known I was going to have to stand before Jesus like this, I would have been a full-on total psycho Christian!

Ashamed and embarrassed, I slowly looked up at Jesus. I was afraid to see the expression on his face. I lifted my head slowly until I expected to catch his eye, but he wasn't looking at me. He was staring at the scorched earth, blankly. He seemed deep in thought, like he was in a disappointed daydream. Then suddenly, he snapped out of it. He looked up at me.

Whatever had happened, Jesus seemed to have got it out of his mind. Then moving his arms lovingly towards me, he spoke. In a loud, almost stereo voice, he said, 'Becky!'

I lightened up a bit. I'd never particularly liked my name. But now it sounded beautiful to me!

And then he said it again, 'Becky, *Come, you who are blessed by my Father; take your inheritance, the kingdom prepared for you since the creation of the world.*' [1]

Trumpets sounded and the entire stadium erupted in noise. I'd been aware that there were people around me, but only now did I look around and see them all on their feet cheering as if a goal had been scored.

Then the angel who had brought out my books came towards me again. Sinking his huge warm hand into mine, he led me off, to Jesus' right-hand side, down a tunnel.

The euphoria and noise died down. They were all waiting for the next person. As suddenly as my 'turn' had arrived, it had gone. I felt as if I'd lost something, as if I'd blown my chance. I couldn't cope. Something inside me snapped. I broke free from the angel's hand and ran back across the open space towards the throne. I shouted out, 'Jesus, I'll make up for it. I'll really serve you in heaven!'

I'd almost got to the platform when the angel caught me, and put both arms round me. He said, 'Come on, you'll enjoy him for ever in heaven. Besides, it's too late! You can't earn any rewards in heaven. They can only be earned on earth.'

---

1. Matthew 25:34.

I'd caused a scene.

He led me back. We stood at the tunnel entrance and I calmed down a bit. For a few minutes, I said nothing. I was trying to make sense of it all.

Shaken and confused, I had to know what had just happened. I looked up at the angel, whose face shone.

'Where are you going?' I asked.

'Going? We are going to heaven, Becky!' his voice was cool, like Jesus' but not quite as true and clear.

'Can we stay here for a moment?'

'Sure,' the angel said. He sensed the intensity of the moment. It seemed as fresh to him as it was to me.

I just wanted time to think. I couldn't cope with going any further. I wanted to understand where I was. I looked back at Jesus into his warm inviting face, which I could now see in profile as I viewed him and the raised platform side-on.

The empty, gutted feeling I'd had in the pit of my stomach was a deep sense that what had just happened to me was some sort of appraisal of my life. It seemed clear that the books being burned up represented what my life had added up to. I already knew I'd let Jesus down on earth. I felt ashamed of myself.

'Can we watch the next one?' I asked.

'Are you serious?' the angel replied, as if I'd asked a question that he'd never been asked before. 'You don't want to go straight to heaven?'

I did, but I couldn't get the sight of the blackened earth out of my mind.

'OK,' the angel said.

We looked back into the stadium. Who was next?

A girl who looked about my age came down the escalator. It was like watching what happened to me again. Jesus found her name too in his book, and a similar number of books were brought out in the same way, and placed at her feet.

Then, in one graceful movement, Jesus took the torch and swooped it down on her books. Then whoosh! With a bang, they caught fire as if they'd been doused in petrol.

So far, her turn had been exactly the same as mine, but as the smoke began to clear, a murmur of excitement went through the crowd. Some of them began pointing. I felt uneasy. One by one they began to gasp and applaud. Soon they were all on their feet. They were pointing at something sparkling in front of this girl. What was it? She bent down and picked it up.

It was a crown! She held it up in triumph. It was gold and silver with different-coloured jewels all over it, and each time she moved, it flickered and shone, reflecting shimmering rays of Jesus' light back towards him.

This was high drama. Holding the crown in the palms of her outstretched hands, she knelt down. Then lowering herself further, she slowly prostrated herself on the ground before Jesus, while keeping the crown off the floor and placing it at his feet.

The crown was almost as big as the stack of books had been! I gazed at it as it sparkled in the light. Then Jesus got up out of his chair and put his arms under hers. Effortlessly, he lifted her up and when she regained her balance, he placed the crown she'd tried to give him on her head! Awesome!

There was more cheering and waving in the crowd, the noise was intense, then Jesus' beautiful voice sliced through it. He said, 'Emma, *Come, you who are blessed by my Father; take your inheritance, the kingdom prepared for you since the creation of the world.*'[1]

I stared blankly. I felt so ashamed of myself. I knew that Jesus loved me just as much, but I'd done so little for him.

Shrieking over the thundering crowd noise, I said to the angel, 'I want to go back.'

'What do you mean?'

'I want to go back and do something more for Jesus.'

'You don't have to. You've made it. You're blameless. You're forgiven. No one will ever be any more forgiven than you are right now. He loves you just as much as her. You know that!'

'But I want to go back!'

'I'm sorry, you can't.'

'OK, well I'll try and impress him here.'

'Becky, I've already told you, you cannot earn any rewards here.'

Rewards! That was it, rewards. That was what the crown was all about!

The angel continued, 'Look. Surely you've understood by now that this is Judgement Day: the day of rewards and punishments. But there's no punishment for you here, Becky.

---

1. Matthew 25:34.

Jesus was punished in your place when he was crucified. Your sins were dealt with there. You trusted in Jesus as your substitute. He took the punishment for your sins when he died on the cross. *There is now no condemnation for those who are in Christ Jesus.*[1]

I looked over at the Emma girl.

The angel could see my train of thought. He said, 'Hey, you're both forgiven sinners. You're both loved equally. She's not any more right with God than you are. You're both justified by grace through faith alone. She's not any more accepted than you are.'

I knew it, but Jesus had been looking for something to reward. And I'd produced nothing.

'Please show me this in the Bible,' I asked the angel, assuming there must be one around somewhere. 'If you're sure,' he said, and came back from the platform with a box.

We sat down on the ground next to the tunnel exit from the stadium. The angel opened the box, and producing a black Bible he began to flick through the pages. 'Well, there are lots of verses that provide an angle on this. Here's one: *Man is destined to die once, and after that to face judgment.*'[2]

That's everyone! Me included! It began to dawn on me what this meant. The angel could see it in my eyes. 'You thought only non-Christians got judged, didn't you?'

I did. 'Christians get judged too,' I said, feeling the need to

---

1. Romans 8:1.
2. Hebrews 9:27.

speak the words out and somehow face up to reality. 'If I'd known that, I would have lived differently. I would have been mega.'

The angel had been searching for something in the Bible. He'd now found whatever he'd been looking for.

'OK, how about this? In the New Testament, the apostle Paul explains to some Christians, *For we must all appear before the judgment seat of Christ, that each one may receive what is due to him for the things done while in the body, whether good or bad.*' [1]

'That is the judgement seat, right?' I said, pointing to the stage.

'Right!'

'And the judgement is with fire, right?'

'Right! Again, Paul refers to this Judgement Day in the New Testament, when he talks about himself building people together as a church, with Jesus as the foundation of the building. Then he goes on to give this warning: *If any man builds on this foundation using gold, silver, costly stones, wood, hay or straw, his work will be shown for what it is, because the Day will bring it to light. It will be revealed with fire, and the fire will test the quality of each man's work. If what he has built survives, he will receive his reward. If it is burned up, he will suffer loss; he himself will be saved, but only as one escaping through the flames.*' [2]

---

1. 2 Corinthians 5:10.
2. 1 Corinthians 3:12–15

I was shocked. Was this really in the Bible?

'You're an angel, right?' I said. 'You've got to tell the truth, right?' He nodded. 'This is what's happened to me, isn't it?'

The angel looked more serious. 'Well, yes,' he answered.

'I've made it by the skin of my teeth, haven't I?'

The angel replied, 'No, you've made it by the blood of Jesus like everyone else. But perhaps in these Bible verses Paul has in mind a man who builds himself a house. Then one night he wakes up to find that his house is on fire. He runs out into the street and escapes from the flames, but as he stands in the road in his underpants, looking back at the house he built, he sees everything he has worked for go up in flames. In that sense, he suffers loss. He's still alive. He is saved, but only as one escaping through the flames.'

This might sound like a lot of Bible-talk to you, but from where we were sitting I could still see the patch of scorched earth where my books had been. These verses in 1 Corinthians were making a lot of sense. Taking the Bible, I read the passage over and over. (On earth I found it a struggle to read the Bible – now I couldn't put it down!)

I stared back at Jesus.

Here's the deal: I had just experienced Judgement Day. For me, the fire had not revealed any gold, silver or costly stones, and certainly not a crown like Emma's. The fire had revealed nothing much. I'd done nothing for Jesus.

The most galling thing was that I wanted to go back and live my life over again, but I couldn't! This was unlike anything else. For example, I remembered how disappointed

I'd been when I'd failed my driving test, but at least I had been able to retake and pass! Then I thought of crashing the car last summer with my friend Rachel – but it was repaired, better than ever! Those setbacks were reversible, but this judgement which really mattered, wasn't!

My ambition was to give Jesus something special, but I couldn't. Emma had been able to present a crown to Jesus. I would never be able to.

I wanted to try and sort out in my mind what I'd learned so far. 'Could you write it all down for me?' I asked the angel.

'What?'

'Anywhere will do,' I said. 'Please can you write down … **"Point One: Christians get judged too!"**'

He walked back towards the platform, and after talking to another very tall angel, he came back holding a classy ink pen. Opening the inside cover of his Bible he then wrote what I'd asked him to at the top of the blank page. But immediately underneath he added, '**Point Two: But it's not a judgement for sin. There's no punishment for Christians when they die, only rewards.**'

'OK,' I said, 'let me try and do some more. Keep writing. How about this: **Point Three: Some Christians get more rewards than others. And Point Four: The more you do for Jesus on earth, the more rewards you get. And Point Five: You can only earn rewards on earth, not in heaven.**'

He nodded and wrote them down.

I finally understood it. Of course, I'd heard that stuff about Christians having houses or mansions in heaven and that some might have bigger mansions than others, but my attitude was 'So what? I don't care about how big my house is, I'll just be happy to be there. Skid row in heaven can't be that much of a dive, can it?' That summed me up.

But being judged was like having to sit my A levels six months early with no warning and no time to revise. I wasn't ready and I'd blown my chances. If only I'd known I was only going to live for 18 years. I would have made every day count, just like Emma … Hang on! … She couldn't have known she was going to die young either … That means she must have lived ready!

I turned round and looked straight at Emma. She wasn't particularly good-looking. She was young and ordinary. I was curious. I thought, 'Maybe she earned so many rewards because she lived in one of those countries where you get persecuted.' I knew there were some countries where your family disown you if you get baptized. Maybe she'd been imprisoned for her faith? Maybe she'd been tortured because she wouldn't deny Jesus?

To be honest, this possibility comforted me! I'm talking about Emma being persecuted. Why? Because I'd always reckoned that if I'd lived in one of those countries, it might have given me the kick up the backside I needed!

Who knows, if the cost had been higher, if I'd had to sacrifice big time on day one, I might have risen to the challenge! It's all or nothing in those countries. If I'd had to lose everything even to become a Christian, I might have been thoroughly sold out and radical. As it was, I hedged my bets.

I knew it was cheeky, but I had to find out where Emma was from. I asked the angel whether he knew. 'Oh yes, I looked at her books,' he said. 'She's British. In fact, she's from the same town as you.'

I crumbled cross-legged on the ground, head in my hands.

I now had to face the facts. In all likelihood, God had given Emma and me the same deal. But she'd served him faithfully, and I hadn't. There were no excuses left for me to explore. I was angry at myself. I said over and over again, 'My sins are forgiven, and yet I suffer loss. It's so pathetic!' I picked up the angel's pen, opened his Bible and wrote, **'Point Six: Some Christians are saved, but still suffer loss! On Judgement Day, Jesus will find nothing he can reward. These Christians make it to heaven, but they'll have nothing to show for their lives on earth.'**

I put the pen down and closed the book. I'd been a blob for Jesus. A spiritual couch potato.

The angel, however, was still trying to think of ways to encourage me. 'Becky, this may not console you,' he said, 'but let me try to explain further what's just happened to you.'

'Please, yes. Talk to me,' I said.

The angel went on, 'Becky, I think the problem you had on the old earth was that you didn't grasp how amazing God's grace is! Before you'd done anything either good or bad, he'd chosen you, and you were his delight, his treasure. You were accepted, loved, forgiven and blameless to start with.

'In his eyes, you were holy even when you were back-sliding! But you didn't really understand that, so whenever you sinned, you got down on yourself and got into a rut of being discouraged and hacked off. You thought God loved you but didn't like you! It's such a shame! You were a born winner without realizing it! You were given a fantastic free gift but never opened the letter because you thought that somehow you had to earn it.

'That's why you didn't enjoy the Christian life more. And things went from bad to worse. Your life ended up a bit like this. ... Imagine God is an architect and he chooses you as a builder. He draws up a wonderful plan, but you disobey his instructions; you build what suits you. You even bring in your own materials instead of his.'

As the angel continued talking, I was staring into the roof of the stadium, and the angel's words started bringing things back to my memory.

Scene One: I remembered when I first got excited about God five years before (I'd only pretended to before then). It was at a summer conference thing. It was the first time I felt I was not leaning on my parents' faith, but had a faith of my own. The whole week I was walking on air, but back at home, it all evaporated in the first month. When I didn't feel the goosebumps any more, I seemed to forget about what God wanted.

But how did it happen? I never ever thought to myself, 'I'll just drift a bit.' The truth is that when following Jesus became a bit routine, when the novelty wore off, when I didn't feel his presence all the time, I just drifted.

I'd been so stupid! God wasn't withdrawing from me; he

wanted me to obey him whether I felt him or not! Becky, you idiot! It's like when my dad took the stabilizers off my bike, or when he first made me swim without armbands. My dad wasn't being cruel; he was being kind. In the same way, God was trying to help me grow up and trust him, but I thought he'd left me. I stopped reading the Bible and started watching things on TV I shouldn't have. (When I was 14, I'd stay up late when my parents were in bed and watched, well, everything I could.) That was the start of it.

Then as in a dream – Scene Two: I saw myself as a 14-year-old, alone in the lounge. The camera panned to the other side of the room and I left the frame. I saw all Mum's cushions, my coffee mug, the crummy pictures on the walls I so hated, and then – to my horror – there was Jesus, standing in the room opposite me! He was standing up, pencil in hand, at an architect's desk. His arm was rapidly moving back and forth across the desk. I saw over his shoulder. He was rubbing out his plans for a building. Then his face softened and he started redrawing the building with some alterations. This so appalled me that I woke up with a start.

The angel was still beside me and I grabbed him: 'I've got to ask you. Did I blow God's best plan for me by sinning?'

'I don't know,' the angel replied. 'The important thing is that all your sin is forgiven and, Becky, in just a moment we'll be in heaven. Then you'll forget it too. You won't be able to remember any sin.'

'But sins have consequences!'

'Not in heaven they don't. Thanks to Jesus!'

'But they do on earth!'

'Well, if a Christian is living selfishly as she pleases, she probably won't be doing things that Jesus can reward.[1] Just as some Christians get into the habit of storing up treasures in heaven, others get into bad habits and don't.'

I asked the angel to write down word for word what he'd just said as Point Seven.

I pictured Jesus again as the architect. What did he plan for me in the first place? Now my mind really was racing.

There were so many other times I'd deliberately failed to follow his plans. I'd rebelled against my parents. I'd done things with boys I knew I shouldn't. I'd been jealous and spiteful. I'd never stood up for Jesus at school. I knew what I hadn't done for him.

Then I was back in my dream.

Scene Three: Now, I was 17 years old and in my bedroom ready to go out. I was going nowhere as a Christian by this stage, and the church youth group bored me. I was off out and somehow God wasn't part of my nights out with my mates. I could see myself looking into my bedroom mirror, and as I stared into it, there was Jesus sitting on my bed! This time I could see straight away that he was drawing. Again, he was rubbing out a picture, and scaling it down into something much smaller.

Scary, isn't it! Talk about being sobered up!

But why hadn't I lived 100 per cent for God? Emma

---

1. 2 Timothy 2:21.

seemed to have managed it. Even 50 per cent would have been something. I reflected long and hard about this.

My answer? It must be because I thought I'd miss out. I wanted to have fun and enjoy myself. I wanted to be liked and I wanted to be like the others. What could be wrong with that? It's more fun to swim with the tide than battle against it. I thought living for God wouldn't be worth it. Being a Christian meant not doing things I wanted to do.

But then a shocking thought hit me. If I'd believed for a moment that my sin would land me in hell, I would have lived like an angel! Yes, just think about it for a moment. It was because I knew I was forgiven that I felt safe to continue as I was. Yuk! How gross! I'd used God's continual forgiveness as a trampoline to sin again and again, all the time knowing I'd got my ticket to heaven.

Living for myself had made sense on earth, but here, sitting with an angel and looking Jesus in the face, it made no sense at all. I felt thoroughly ashamed.

Then I pictured myself at church, with my hands lifted up. Every Sunday I joined in songs that said, 'I love you, Lord,' or something like that. Jesus must have been watching me, saying, 'What? You love me? But we never spend any time together! Do you realize what you're saying?'

My Christianity was a compromise. What if I'd treated a boyfriend like I'd treated God? I would have said, 'Simon, I love you, and I'm basically yours, but I really want to spend one day a week with Mark. I know that's not ideally what you're looking for, but it's the best I can manage at the moment. Sorry. That's just the way it is.'

It was time for the next person to be judged.

'This man was a pastor,' the angel said. 'In fact he was a major Christian leader in your country. He was extremely well respected by Christians everywhere. Jesus touched many people through this minister.'

The 'minister' man was old and looked impressive and dignified. I was startled by how many books were brought out – probably three times as many as mine and Emma's put together. I marvelled at what kind of crown the fire would reveal. I was genuinely thrilled to think how much glory this man's life would bring to Jesus.

Again, Jesus swooped down with his torch. The same flash of fire followed. Then the smoke lifted and there were gasps all around the stadium. The fire had revealed … nothing! The crowd gasped. The man sank to his knees and began crying.

He then started rummaging around in the dirt. What for? He obviously found something there, because he scooped up some shiny bits of metal, and cupping his hands he presented them to Jesus. It was a pathetic sight.

The angel said to me, 'This is the worst kind of humiliation.'

'Why didn't he get a crown?' I asked.

'Becky, this minister did lots for God, but he really wanted to impress people. He had impure motives and the fire burns up all impurities. Those scraps of gold and silver he scooped up represent the little bit he did with pure motives.'

The angel was determined to show me this in the Bible too. He flicked over a few pages and got me to read it out loud:

'Therefore judge nothing before the appointed time; wait till the Lord comes. He will bring to light what is hidden in darkness and will expose the motives of men's hearts. At that time each will receive his praise from God. [1]

'So this old minister got very little reward?'

'He didn't get much praise from Jesus, but he got lots from people on earth. Jesus said, *Be careful not to do your "acts of righteousness" before men, to be seen by them. If you do, you will have no reward from your Father in heaven.*' [2]

By now the minister had been helped towards the tunnel to heaven. He was no more than a few yards from me. He was talking to the angel who was supporting him as he stumbled along.

Then the old man collapsed to the ground and said to his angel, 'I was so worried that my sin would find me out on earth – but if I'd thought how much worse it was being found out here, I'd have confessed every sin to my congregation in seconds.'

Exposed before Jesus!

My angel listened in too. Then turning to another Bible verse, he said to me, *'Nothing in all creation is hidden from God's sight. Everything is uncovered and laid bare before the eyes of him to whom we must give account.'* [3]

It was chilling. I picked up the pen and wrote, **'Point Eight: Everyone who does stuff for Jesus with impure**

---

1. 1 Corinthians 4:5.
2. Matthew 6:1.
3. Hebrews 4:13.

motives will be exposed. Everyone trying to impress people will be found out.'

By now a middle-aged woman was standing before Jesus. Again a very large number of books were brought out. When Jesus set them ablaze, once more nothing was left except a few stones and fragments of gold. The woman was astonished.

As she was led away, she asked, 'What happened to my crown?'

'You lost it,' her angel replied, as he brushed my shoulder, taking her to heaven.

I swung round and asked my angel, 'Hang on, how did she lose her crown?'

'She started off brilliantly. She served Jesus wholeheartedly. Jesus set her free from a negative self-image, obsessive thinking, overanalysing everything, bitterness, self-pity, envy and lots more. She had a stunning testimony and through her faithfulness to Jesus she earned many rewards, but in the last five years of her life she fell back into serious sin.'

He said: 'If only she'd heeded these warnings: *Watch out that you do not lose what you have worked for, but that you may be rewarded fully.*[1] And Jesus himself promised, *I am coming soon. Hold on to what you have, so that no-one will take your crown.*'[2]

'I don't get it,' I said.

'Well, if you're playing football, it's the result at the final whistle that matters.'

---

1. 2 John 8.
2. Revelation 3:11.

'You mean she was 1–0, up in injury time, but still lost 2–1.'

The angel obviously thought this was a bit flippant, but at least I'd understood it. I took the pen again. **'Point Nine: Watch out!'** I wrote. **'Some Christians may lose the rewards they earned.'**

Then the angel said, 'Now, let's get you to the Marriage Supper.'

'The Marriage Supper?'

'Yes, I'm taking you to heaven.'

'How about two more?' I asked. 'Let me see just two more being judged.'

'OK, just two more,' the angel agreed, but was still a bit bemused. I can't explain my curiosity about judgement, because I was itching to get into heaven.

Anyway, the next person was another white teenage girl, just like me and Emma. She arrived on the escalator. But as soon as her feet touched the ground, Jesus said, *'Depart from me, you who are cursed, into the eternal fire prepared for the devil and his angels.'*[1]

I felt a sharp stab in my stomach. I was totally shocked and very scared by what Jesus had just said. This was the same Jesus who'd welcomed me!

'No! Wait!' the girl replied. 'It's me – Nicola. You've made a mistake. I know I wasn't religious, but I was basically a good person.'

---

1. Matthew 25:41.

'I never knew you,' Jesus said. *'Away from me!'* [1]

And that was it! In seconds, she was gone. No books, no fire, no crowns, no blackened earth either. She was whisked off by angels to the other side of the stadium. For ever!

My heart sank. 'Mr Angel, is she going to hell?'

'Well, she can't bring her sin into heaven,' he replied. 'Jesus himself said, *Nothing impure will ever enter it.*' [2]

'Nicola was a nasty piece of work, right?'

'Well, she was a sinner who hadn't received forgiveness, but she was kinder and more considerate than many other people.'

I couldn't think of anything to say in response to this. Even a relatively good person was too impure for heaven!

The angel repeated: *Nothing impure will ever enter it.* [3]

Don't get me wrong – it made sense. Heaven had to be pure. A polluted heaven was impossible. And if Nicola had done half the sinning I had, she could hardly claim to deserve a place there! Jesus' judgement seemed fair to me, but it was still frightening.

Until now, I'd only seen Christians get judged: me, Emma, the old boy minister bloke and the middle-aged lady. Seeing Nicola, I began to realize just how serious our sin is. Here sin seemed so out of place, so repulsive. Yet on earth, it seemed normal.

Sin, for me, was mostly in the mind, especially sexual sins. We

1. Matthew 7:23.
2. Revelation 21:27.
3. Revelation 21:27.

were supposed to avoid temptation, but I rather enjoyed it. *'Flee also youthful lusts,'*[1] our inspiring youth pastor had told us, but they were so juicy! I would get as close as I possibly could, and then try and pull away at the last minute, by which stage, I sometimes didn't feel like pulling away.

Now, I felt awful about what I had watched, what I had said, what I had thought, but also what I had done and where I had done it; somehow it all now seemed so disgusting. I knew where the boundaries were, but time and again I'd go right up to the edge of the cliff and then walk along it. Surprise, surprise, I regularly fell over the edge into sin. I'd feel bad for a few days, but then there was always forgiveness.

Nicola's sins may not have been as bad as mine, but they'd still landed her in hell! I should have been joining her. I deserved it as much as she did.

I felt a sudden rush of gratitude to Jesus. I could see him on the platform. 'Sweet Jesus,' I said, looking at him, 'you're my Saviour!'

The angel smiled and said, *'God made him who had no sin to be sin for us, so that in him we might become the righteousness of God.'*[2]

'Does that mean I am really righteous?'

'Of course you are. And not just now – you have been ever since you believed. In fact God planned it even before you were born! God made Jesus who never sinned to become sin

---

1. 2 Timothy 2:22, AV.
2. Corinthians 5:21.

on the cross. You became as righteous as God is! It's amazing! Surely someone explained this to you? It's the grace of God.'

'Tell me more,' I said. 'Tell me more stuff about grace.'

'He himself bore our sins in his body on the tree.' [1]

And then I thought of one myself, from my Sunday school days. I said triumphantly: *'God demonstrates his own love for us in this: While we were still sinners, Christ died for us.'* [2]

My excitement was immediately cooled by another thought: 'Did anyone ever tell Nicola about the cross? Did anyone tell her that she was hell-bound? Did anyone ever tell her that *God so loved the world that he gave his one and only Son, that whoever believes in him shall not perish but have eternal life?'* [3] (That's my only other memory verse – you've got them both now.) Did anyone ever tell her?

Before I had time to ask the angel whether Nicola heard about Jesus, the next person was entering the stadium. My last! I'd said two more. Nicola was the first, this was going to be the second.

'We're off to the Marriage Supper after this,' the angel reminded me.

Who was going to be the last person I'd see judged? I felt a nervous excitement. Would they be heaven-bound or hell-bound? In seconds we'd know.

It was a bloke. Again a teenager. 'Hang on,' I said to the

---

1. 1 Peter 2:24.
2. Romans 5:8.
3. John 3:16.

angel. 'That looks like … um … No! It couldn't be! It was a kid I knew from college … Daniel Adams! I looked at his face, which I'd seen all through school and college. Then a picture flashed into my mind … the sick, motionless boy in the car wreckage. Oh no! … That was him! That was Daniel Adams! Now I recognized him. It was definitely Daniel in the car and Daniel in front of me. It all fell into place – he'd died moments after I did, and now he was being judged.

But was Daniel a Christian?

Of course he wasn't! No, he was just a normal kid at school.

Oh no! … He was going to go to hell. I turned away, clasped the angel's hand and said, 'I've seen enough, let's go!'

'But you wanted to see two more, and this one hasn't finished,' the angel replied.

'I've changed my mind! One's enough. I can't stand it,' I said as we walked away down the tunnel. We were leaving the stadium. My steps quickened. My heart quickened.

Daniel was going to go to hell! Why couldn't a Christian have told him about Jesus?

A pause. I stopped. I could have told him! I may have been the only person who could have told him! I could have told Daniel Adams about Jesus and forgiveness and judgement. I had the chance, and I didn't! Now, it was too late! I screamed 'No!' and spun round in the tunnel and began running back towards Daniel.

The angel grabbed me. 'Becky, Jesus will judge justly.'

'Please let me go, you don't understand!' I struggled, trying to get free. 'I knew this one. It's Daniel Adams. He's going to go to hell and it's my fault.'

'It's not your fault if he goes to hell. It's his own sin that will take him there if that's where he ends up.'

'Look, he died in the same accident as me. He wasn't ready. Please let me go.'

The angel would not let me go back. He held me tight in the tunnel, like a wrestler giving someone a bear hug.

How could Daniel have known about Jesus? He would never have seen anything distinctive in me. He would never have seen something authentic. He needed to see a clear line between a Christian and a non-Christian. He probably didn't have a clue about Jesus and the cross. I had failed him. I was so gutted.

Of course I didn't go round telling people at school about Jesus. I wanted people to like me, I didn't want to be rejected. Besides I was scared. OK, that's not true; I wasn't scared, but I wanted to have respect. I didn't want people to think I was sad, or a pain. I just wanted to be normal.

Incredible isn't it! Saved from hell by Jesus, but I told hardly anyone who needed to know. Now it seemed so stupid, yet on earth it was just the way I was. Somehow religious, spiritual things didn't seem real enough for me to talk about them.

Everyone else was concerned with what others thought of them, and I was too. I bet Emma told everyone. She was probably dead to what people thought of her. That's what I should have been: dead to the world, but alive for Jesus.

Now I was dead, I felt like I had Daniel Adams's blood on my hands.

What was I taking to heaven with me? No possessions, no reputation, and no Daniel Adams. Nothing. The only thing I could have taken with me was people. I'm sure Emma was taking many, but I wasn't.

But imagine if I'd been arrested for something. Imagine if the punishment was three years in prison or £3,000 bail. If a friend had sold everything they had and raised the £3,000, I would have done anything for them. Yet Jesus saved me from hell, and I was too cool to tell people what he'd done for me!

I thought of Jesus' face when he saw my books burned up. I thought of him looking disappointedly at the blackened earth.

'For a moment, Jesus was ashamed of me, wasn't he?' I asked the angel.

He replied, 'Jesus said: *If anyone is ashamed of me and my words in this adulterous and sinful generation, the Son of Man will be ashamed of him when he comes in his Father's glory with the holy angels.*[1] But Becky, you are not responsible for whatever happens to Daniel. He will be judged justly. Now let that sink in. It will comfort you. No one is going to be punished unjustly.

'Judgement is God's responsibility and not yours. God is in charge of who hears about Jesus. It's his grace that saves, not your efforts or obedience. If God's decided to save someone, he'll do it with or without your help. He runs the universe and salvation belongs to him, not you, Becky! He is sovereign.

---

1. Mark 8:38.

He's the King of the universe.'

There was comfort in this; it did help. God runs the universe. He calls the shots, not me. I felt better, steadier, more peaceful. But Jesus having to scale down the plan for my life still bothered me, as I thought about the many opportunities I'd missed to share his love with others.

We started walking out of the stadium of judgement for ever.

One thing I knew: because Jesus died for me, and because he'd enabled me to believe it, I was going to heaven not hell. I opened the angel's Bible and wrote some more words: '**Point Ten: Whatever rewards Christians may or may not receive, they still go to heaven.**'

I closed my eyes and tried to imagine – what would heaven be like?

3

ecstatic – the red-hot christian

Well done, good and faithful servant! You have been faithful with a few things; I will put you in charge of many things. Come and share your master's happiness! (Matthew 25:21)

'Phew! What a scorcher!' A sizzling summer day was the radio forecast. Perhaps I should go upstairs and change. I could wear my vest-top. That was it – I'd decided. I sat eating Frosties, with my hair up in a towel. It was the second day of the holiday job. Data entry. Not very exciting, but I'd had some excellent opportunities to talk to some of the other students already, one of whom I'd been at primary school with, or so we found out yesterday!

In our department there were four of us, all back from our first year at university, trying to earn some extra cash for a few weeks before going away. My dad was taking me into work, an insurance firm in the town centre. He was going that way.

The day before, he'd been away overnight and I'd caught the bus in. But today he was only going to Birmingham and back, which for him was a very short trip. Just like old times, I climbed in and he gave me a lift into town.

It was fun to talk to my dad again, as I hadn't seen him since the Christmas holidays. My parents were away over Easter, so my sister and I had had the house to ourselves.

It was like being a kid again when I talked to Dad, except now I was 20 and we had so much to catch up on. He'd ask me in detail about the books I was studying (I was doing English Literature) because he said he was trying to catch up on all the schooling he'd missed. (That's a story in itself.) Anyway, he always had funny stories about where he'd been abroad and people he'd met in obscure parts of the world. I was telling him all about term and what God had been doing in our hall, where we'd seen two people become Christians the Sunday after my last end-of-year exam.

We pulled onto the dual carriageway. It really was going to be hot. Dad was sweating. I reached for the fan. Then I remembered, there was no air-conditioning in this thing.

Opening the glove compartment slowly, I asked, 'What tapes have you got in here, Dad?'

Before he could answer, we suddenly swerved violently. Then an almighty thud! … The seatbelt cracked tight across my chest. We'd hit a car in front and bounced off.

'Oh no!'

Then an even bigger jerk as we were shunted from behind. It was frightening. Dad was screaming, 'Get out of the way!'

Then I saw her. There was a girl right there on the pavement! We were sure to hit her! I couldn't bear to look. 'Aaagh!'

And that's the last I remember. I don't think I went through the windscreen. Maybe I just hit my head on the dashboard. You sometimes got thrown around a bit, but until then I'd always felt so safe up there in the cab.

Momentary blackness. Silence. Peace.

I promise you I was only in darkness for a second, and then I definitely felt something. My eyelids fluttered. A rush of sensation. My eyes sprang open. Oh Jesus! Is this it? I was conscious.

I was moving. I looked down at my feet. They were stationary. I was standing up. Correction – I was standing and moving at the same time – on an escalator!

'Yes, Lord! Yes, Lord!' I wanted to shout it out, but I only whispered it. Was I really dead?

I wanted confirmation. I wanted to see something that couldn't possibly be normal life. As I rose further, I felt more and more confident that this was definitely not a dream.

As I looked down, I saw a wispy swirl of colour, and then what looked like the back of a stadium. There was a murmur of crowd noise. I was so excited!

'Yes!' I screamed. 'King Jesus! This is it!'

You'd think there would be some sort of period for adjustment and reflection for me to chew on thoughts like 'Oh, so I die young.' Or 'Why me?' How about, 'Why did you take me when I could have done so much more for you?' or a sense of loss like 'Oh, so I'm not going to get married

Lord,' or 'Oh, so I'm never going to have children'? But not a bit of it! I was having too much fun to think any of these things. I just remember yelling my head off! I haven't made so much noise since I last went on a roller coaster.

I climbed and climbed over the back of the stadium. This was so cool. I promise you, you'll love it when it's your turn.

Any second I'd see him. I was so far up by now that I felt like I was in a glider cockpit looking down on the circular stadium. From here it looked like a volcano about to erupt with glorious light pouring out of the centre of it. I started to descend, ever so gently. All the colours of the rainbow were flashing up out of the stadium. Not lasers. Not fireworks either. A sort of mixture, but better than both!

Any second now ... face to face with *the* light, my heart's desire. This was undiluted pleasure. Sheer indulgence.

There was a whoosh of groundrush as I touched down inside the stadium like a parachutist. On landing, I was blinded by dazzling whiteness. Rubbing my eyes, I looked up.

And he was right there! Within touching distance, sitting on a white throne on a huge platform, with head, arms, body. 'Jesus? It's really you, isn't it!' I mouthed, but no sound came out.

His eyes seemed to be on fire. And then he stood up. And with a swish of his white robe, he flashed a flaming torch down to my feet.

I followed the arc of the flame to the books in front of me. Where did those books come from? Then a clap of combustion and a fireball! And I jumped back.

Jesus was looking at my feet and laughing. But why?

Then I realized. Lying on the brown baked earth by my feet, right there before me was a crown.

I'd often tried to picture this scene in my mind's eye, but it was all so much brighter than anything I could have imagined. It was beautiful. It really was a crown, with large jewels and stones and thick gold. What was I doing with the crown jewels? Was this crown really mine? No, it must be his! I picked it up and instinctively fell down in front of him. Everything within me wanted automatically to give Jesus the crown. I placed it at his feet. Then I thought, 'Hang on, isn't this what the 24 elders do in Revelation?' I was just trying to remember what they say or sing as they do it, when I felt a man's heavy hands on my head.

Oh! I felt that!

Jesus had placed the crown on my head! Then he picked me up like a feather. 'Emma,' he spoke, his voice booming, *'Come, you who are blessed by my Father; take your inheritance, the kingdom prepared for you since the creation of the world.'* [1]

Oh yes! I felt his pleasure. I'd felt it before on earth, but this was so exhilarating. I don't know quite what happened next. I think I was a bit intoxicated by it all. I remember going through a tunnel accompanied by what must have been an angel.

And then we were outside the stadium.

I collected my thoughts. What now? Heaven! Life as I

---

1. Matthew 25:34.

knew it was over, and I'd received my reward at judgement. The only thing before me now was sheer pleasure with Jesus and his church! I turned to the angel next to me.

'Are you taking me to heaven?' I asked.

'Oh yes.'

'Where is it?'

'See for yourself!'

I looked around for ... I don't know what. The horizon was filled by a towering mountain, which rose up out of the mist behind the stadium. Beyond it, we could hear the drone of conversation and cheers and singing. We set out walking on a path up the mountain and then broke into a run. With each step the singing became louder and I felt more energy surging through my body. Surely a vast crowd was about to come into view below us when we reached the top of the mountain. When we did, we gasped. Looking down the other side, there were people swarming as far as the eye could see. And right before us, a glorious city descending from above with walls that sparkled!

I'm making it sound like some enormous UFO – but this was no sci-fi flick.

The only other time I'd gasped like this was when we visited the Grand Canyon, but that was sad compared to this.

Everyone was streaming towards the city. Were these really heaven's walls? I'd never really understood the exact sequence of events at death, but I was sure from what I remembered of the book of Revelation that I was watching heaven descending.

As far as the eye could see below us, there were people: one huge mass. I'd never been part of such a surging crowd all moving in the same direction. There was laughter and singing. Every language seemed to blend into one. And I could understand them all. Had the barriers of language been removed?

Then I felt a tap on my shoulder. Turning round, I almost knocked over a girl who I thought I recognized. 'Hi!' I said.

'Emma!' she replied in an emphatic way.

'You know my name!' I was shocked. 'Wow! Have we met?'

'No.' She looked quite drained and was leaning on a huge angel. (I'll tell you about angels if I get the chance. Angels are the business!)

'How do you know my name?'

'Well, I was watching you at judgement, and I saw your books and heard Jesus say your name. I just wanted to say how impressed I was ...'

'Are you sure we haven't met?' I just knew we had.

'Don't think so! I saw you get judged, that's the only reason I know your name, and ...'

Then I realized.

She kept talking, but I stopped listening.

This was the last person I'd seen on earth! Oh Lord! This was the girl we'd run over in the lorry! The girl we'd hit. But ... my heart leapt ... she was a Christian! She was saved! Yes! What were the chances of that? Oh thank you, Jesus! I had to talk to her. But how was she going to react? 'Can we sit down?' I asked.

We both had angels with us, but they looked at each other knowingly and left us as we found our way to a grassy bank. I was desperately keen to find out if this girl was who I thought she was. Everything had gone so quickly from being in the lorry to being judged, and in a few moments, we'd be inside the city. But here I was with this girl. How should I begin?

'This may come as a bit of a surprise,' I said, 'but I've got to ask you something.'

'Oh good,' she replied, 'because I want to ask you something. In fact I'd like to ask you lots of things.'

'First of all, what's your name?'

'Becky Mason.'

'Becky, did you die in a car accident?'

'Yes, except I wasn't in a car. I was just walking to college. I was hit by a lorry.'

'Becky, did you see the driver of the lorry?'

'Yes, briefly.'

'Did he have a passenger with him?'

'Maybe. It was only a split second.'

'Becky, my dad was the driver of the lorry and I was in the passenger seat.'

Silence. But she was smiling.

'Becky, I'm telling you that we killed you. How can you be smiling?'

'Emma, I'm just so thrilled that you're saved,' she said.

Perhaps you were expecting me to tell you that she freaked. She didn't. I then explained it all in detail, about my dad and all our family being born again. You might also expect that when it all calmed down, she asked a lot of 'Why me?' questions, but she didn't! (By the way, neither of us knew how the accident had happened.) We both just felt so grateful to Jesus that he'd saved us.

The funny thing was that as we talked, several other people gathered round, and listened in! I wondered what these people were so interested in, but as I looked at them, I saw they weren't looking at me. They were staring at the crown on my head.

'How did you get it?' Becky asked.

Then like a chorus before someone bursts into song in a musical, they all echoed one after another, 'Tell us, please.'

'Well, I don't know exactly, but I can tell you a bit about my life.'

'Oh yes please,' Becky said. 'I want to know how a normal girl in our town ended up with that crown.'

Then, everyone started talking excitedly at the same time. (Those who'd gathered round had all been teenagers at the beginning of the twenty-first century, like me.) Then, one by one they fell silent.

I began my testimony feeling a bit self-conscious. 'I was brought up in a Christian home. I believed all the right things, but I was just coasting along. I had a fairly low opinion of myself. I thought I was ugly – you know the classic inferiority complex thing. I took it out on other people. Very cutting, sarcastic. I either liked you or I didn't, and if I didn't then you were a real hate target. I had serious attitude. I was a right cow sometimes. I wasn't content to stick the knife in – I had to give it a couple of twists. But it made me more and more dissatisfied. I didn't aim for much spiritually and didn't achieve very much. Then, when I was 15, I went on a Christian camp and I really understood the grace of God for the first time.'

'What exactly do you mean by that?' someone asked.

'Well, I suppose until then, being a Christian had just seemed like an endless losing battle. I felt that I should be doing things to please God, but I didn't want to do them. So I was stuck.'

'But that's just how I felt,' Becky said. 'So what changed?'

'Like I said, the grace of God. At that camp, I really understood that I could never earn my way to heaven with any amount of holy living. So I stopped trying. I just looked to Jesus and started believing all those Bible verses that say that he is our holiness and that salvation is a totally free gift. You have to accept it. You can't earn it, nor can you pay God back for it. He doesn't want you to. It's a free gift! So my favourite verse is *For it is by grace you have been saved, through faith – and this not from yourselves, it is the gift of God – not by works so that no-one can boast.*' [1]

'So believing that cheered you up?' a black guy (called Marcus, I later found out) asked.

'Cheered me up? It made me want to fly and gave me wings too! It just took all the pressure off. So from that day to this, I've been motivated by God's grace. And the funny thing is, I

---

1. Ephesians 2:8–9.

was so delighted and felt so secure that I was loved and accepted on the basis of what Jesus had done for me on the cross, that I ended up wanting to live all out for Jesus after all! I began to think, "If God is for me, who can be against me?"'

'So grace made you want to live for Jesus?' (Marcus again).

I thought of a verse that summed it up nicely. I said, 'How about this? *His grace to me was not without effect. No, I worked harder than all of them – yet not I, but the grace of God that was with me.*[1] So the foundation for everything I've done since leaving that camp has been grace. I'm not striving to please God any more.'

'That verse says, "I worked hard",' Marcus said. 'Would you say you worked hard for Jesus?'

'Well, I realized that when I got to heaven, God wasn't going to ask me what my highest score in Pokémon or Tomb Raider was.'

They laughed. (By now there were about twenty people listening in as I sat next to Becky on the grass bank.)

A boy with slicked-back hair then asked, 'So, if you could have your time over again, isn't there anything you would do differently?'

I thought for a moment. 'I can't think of anything,' I replied.

'You mean you wouldn't change a thing?' he asked, almost incredulous.

'No, I wouldn't change a thing. From the age of 15

---

1. 1 Corinthians 15:10.

onwards, I gave it my best shot. I wasn't perfect, and I could have done so much more for Jesus, but for the past five years I've given it all I've got.'

'Wow, you really were radical,' he said.

'Do you think so? Let me ask you something: Is it radical for a soldier to obey his commanding officer?' [1]

Silence.

'Answer me this then … If the commanding officer tells a new recruit to jump up out of the trenches and run towards the enemy guns, and the new recruit does it – I ask you, does the commanding officer spill his cup of tea in shock and say, "Wow, that's radical!"? Of course he doesn't! It's not radical for a soldier to obey his commanding officer. That's what he signed up for.'

Becky asked, 'Are you saying that when you become a Christian you can't do what you want to any more?'

'When you become a Christian you die to yourself! And then Christ puts his life in you. Think about the apostle Paul. He said, *I have been crucified with Christ and I no longer live, but Christ lives in me.*' [2]

Becky answered, 'Well, I must admit, I remember sitting in a few church services thinking, "If this is abundant life, if this is knowing God personally, if this is what I was created and predestined for, then it's not up to much!"'

'When we signed up to follow Jesus, we signed our lives

---

1. 2 Timothy 2:4.
2. Galatians 2:20.

away on day one,' I said. 'We gave up our rights. We died, didn't we? That was the whole point, wasn't it? I know some of us didn't realize it, but think of that soldier: he never chooses when to wake up or eat. In fact, he may have his personal preferences denied him at every single stage of his life, but he ends up getting decorated with medals simply for doing what he was told!'

They seemed tremendously impressed by this, but I wasn't satisfied.

'What's wrong with my story about the soldier?' I asked.

No response.

'People can volunteer to be soldiers,' I continued. 'They can apply to serve in the army, but dead people can't volunteer to be made alive.'

More blank expressions. Then one of them said, 'OK, I can see what you're getting at. You're on about us being spiritually dead in our sins before we became Christians.'

'That's right, each one of us was dead. We couldn't choose to live. Without Jesus we were stuffed. *But because of his great love for us, God, who is rich in mercy, made us alive with Christ even when we were dead in transgressions.*[1] It's the grace of God again!'

They all cheered at this, and a few of them hugged each other.

'Or, here's another angle on it,' I said. 'Imagine that every time you sinned against God, you went further and further

---

1. Ephesians 2:4–5.

into debt. It gets so bad that you end up selling yourself into slavery. Or worse still, imagine you were born into slavery, the son of a slave. You're hanging around in the slave market, helpless, and totally unable ever to pay God back. But then God, out of pure love, pays the full price to buy you out of slavery and sets you free for ever! And with what did he pay for us? With what did he redeem us?'

'His blood!' Becky answered.

'That's right. The blood of his own Son! He wrote the cheque in Jesus' blood.' (I loved talking about the blood!) 'So let me give it to you straight: *You are not your own; you were bought at a price.*[1] So you're not just a volunteer soldier. You're more precious to God than that!'

'Thank you, Lord!' one of them shouted. Then we were caught up with a gush of praise, which broke out spontaneously. We all stood up. Then it all kicked off into a play fight and we ended up in a heap. For many of us it was just beginning to sink in that we were going to be face to face with this self-sacrificing Saviour for ever.

And still the questions flowed. A tall blonde-haired boy asked, 'But did you have any problems?'

'Sure. I got opposition from non-Christians, even opposition from Christians. I was seriously ill twice. I passed up lots of opportunities and missed out on relationships I might have enjoyed. We had some real heartaches in my family, but my perspective was "no matter how bad it gets, Emma, one day

---

1. 1 Corinthians 6:20.

it'll be over and you'll be in heaven". I also told myself that if Jesus commanded us not to worry – and worrying was never going to help me anyway – then I'd train myself not to worry.'

'What do you mean, you trained yourself?'

'I taught myself Bible verses and I'd preach to myself whenever I started to get fearful or anxious. I used the promises of God as weapons in an internal mental battle I fought every day!'

'A mental battle! It all sounds pretty serious,' one of them said. 'Did you ever have any fun?'

Before I could answer, Becky said, 'You're not seriously asking that, are you? Look at how she oozes joy. She never would have got that crown by being miserable. Unhappy Christians aren't a great advert for Christianity, are they! She's not being arrogant – it's her humility that's earned her that crown. But we keep asking her in detail about her walk with God, and it's obvious she'd rather we ask her about Jesus. Just look at her face! She's had more fun in her life than the rest of us put together! It's how she lived that we're finding challenging.'

'Look, you've got me all wrong – I was nothing special,' I said. I remembered times when I'd had to make myself rejoice even when I didn't feel like it! Because I was a naturally low person with an inferiority complex, I'd had to learn the secret of being content with my lot in life.[1]

Next they asked me about what opposition I'd received

1. Philippians 4:12.

when talking about Jesus at school and university, but the more we talked, the more I was reminded that the opposition had only spurred me on. It encouraged me that I was making an impression. The real challenge was to persevere with friends who just weren't interested. That's where I could have become discouraged. When I told people how much Jesus had done for me, a typical response was 'That's nice for you but it's not for me.' So I made myself challenge non-Christians, and tell them that a judgement was coming to everyone.

'You must have led many people to Jesus to get that crown.'

'No, I don't know that I did. There were some, but I viewed evangelism as a process because most people we lived with were far from God when we first met them, so I simply prayed that I would be able to help them move closer to faith in Christ, no matter how far away they were.'

At that moment, I remembered something my mum had told me, which was, 'God has called us to be faithful, not successful.' I found that so helpful, even beyond the grave!

Then I thought of something equally important. 'And another thing,' I said, really getting into my stride, 'I realized that the big issue for non-Christians was that they didn't know what a real Christian was. Lots of them had some experience of dry religion, but they needed to see a clear line between what a Christian was and what a non-Christian was. Think of all the people in Britain who thought they'd make it to heaven! They reckoned they were OK, so they didn't see the need to go to church or take Jesus seriously. It really sobered me up to realize that I was the only Bible most of my friends would ever read, so if I didn't live right, if I didn't live holy, what chance was there that they'd meet Jesus through me?

'If I didn't tell them about heaven or hell, I knew I'd never be able to look them in the eye on Judgement Day. I didn't want anyone to say to me, "Emma, if you knew I was going to hell, why didn't you warn me?"'

'You told people about hell, like in normal conversation?' a dark-haired girl asked incredulously.

'Yes.'

'But wasn't that awful and embarrassing and really awkward?'

'Yes it was, but love warns. We warn children away from fires and poisonous pills and dangerous roads because we love them. I couldn't bring myself to talk only about heaven as if everyone goes there no matter what. Jesus frequently warned people that they were in danger of going to hell. Is it really love never to mention hell to people who might be going there?'

More silence.

Another asked: 'So you were totally authentic and distinctive? You never slipped up, like getting drunk or going too far with a boyfriend?'

'I made up my mind at 15 that, by the grace of God, I was going to live for Jesus. And I got aggressive about it. I thought, "Emma, anyone can get drunk. Anyone can sleep around, but it takes a woman of God to stand up under the pressure and say, 'No, I'm living for Jesus!'"'

'So,' the blonde boy asked, 'let's get specific. How much time each day did you spend praying and witnessing to non-Christians?'

'That's not the point,' I said. 'The key thing was that I realized at 15 that I would never have any regrets about time I spent going after God, but I also realized that I would have regrets about wasted time. Besides, I believe that in my generation a relay baton was being passed to us from my parents' generation, and if I dropped it, someone else was going to have to run twice as fast, so I wanted to sprint for the line.[1] That's why I decided to train myself to be godly.[2] It didn't come naturally. Christianity is not automatic.'

Then another girl joined in. 'You talk about being like an athlete or a soldier,' she said. 'But I didn't have any of these battles. I think now that I was asleep really. If the devil can see we're sleeping, he's not likely to wake us up by attacking us!'

'That's right,' I responded. 'The devil's best plan is to keep you asleep. No, scrub that – his best plan of all is to keep you sleeping and then fool you into thinking that you're actually awake and on active service!'

'Exactly,' Becky butted in. 'That's it in a nutshell, isn't it! People like me thought I was further on than I actually was. I thought that because my church was considered lively and happening, I was too.'

Some of them didn't get it. So I put it this way: 'If you bunked off church and went to drunken orgies every weekend, you probably wouldn't think of yourself as an on-fire Christian. But you run the risk of being deceived when you're

---

1. Philippians 3:14.
2. 1 Timothy 4:7.

in church hearing Scripture yet not doing what it says.' [1]

This seemed to really hit home. Then the blonde boy asked, 'You mentioned the devil. Did you think about what the devil might do to try and stop you?'

'Sure. I actually sat down once with a piece of paper and tried to second-guess his strategy! I asked myself, "If I was the devil, where would I attack Emma?"'

'What?' Becky answered. 'Were we supposed to do that?'

'I don't know, but it seemed to me to be common sense. For example, I decided that if I was the devil, I would be extremely subtle and try to undermine Emma's relationship with God, without ever doing it so blatantly that Emma would notice what I was up to.

'I first of all wrote down what I thought my weaknesses were. Then I asked some other people what they thought my weaknesses were. Then I made myself accountable to someone.'

'What do you mean?' a girl with spiky hair asked.

'I got a friend to question me regularly about my weaknesses.'

'It all sounds very intense,' another said.

'It was! Every Monday we met up and she asked me 16 questions about various areas of temptation I might have faced during the previous week.'

At that moment, I heard one girl whisper to another, 'It's like she was in a war!'

'It wasn't like a war. It was war,' [2] I said.

---

1. James 1:22.
2. 2 Corinthians 10:3.

I don't know how long we'd been talking for, but there was a break at this stage as they all started earnest discussions among themselves, and then some wandered off. (I found out why later.)

At this point, Becky took me aside and explained that she'd been shocked and ashamed before Jesus at the judgement seat. She said she hadn't even realized that Christians got judged! The whole thing had come as a complete surprise! The twenty or so others all seemed to have had the same experience of suffering loss of some kind.

'Look, there's no sense of loss in heaven,' I said. 'And no shame either. There's no guilt or tears. Come on, let's go into the city,' I urged them, taking two of them by the hand.

'But what about the martyrs?' said one of the girls.

I stopped. This came out of nowhere. 'What about them?'

She went on, 'Well, we know there's something in the book of Revelation about the Marriage Supper of the Lamb. That's what we've all just been talking about. At the Marriage Supper, we've been told, all the Christians from every century are all together. So what if we find ourselves sitting opposite a martyr? Someone mega-holy; someone who was burned at the stake?'

'Or someone the Romans threw to the lions?' another added.

The blonde boy was clearly the spokesman. He said, 'We'll be so embarrassed! I mean, let's face it, when you have dinner, you tend to talk to whoever you sit with. The martyrs will talk about how they died for Jesus. How they were tortured, but refused to deny Christ. Then they'll ask us,

"How was it for you in Britain in the year 2000? What did you have to contend with? What did you do for Jesus?" Can you imagine! So we wanted to prepare ourselves a bit by talking to you, and hang on … here's another one.'

Before I had a chance to come back on what they'd said, amid much backslapping and congratulations, the ones who'd wandered off returned with a tall gangly looking boy who had on his head a crown very similar to mine. He was extremely jolly and again was about the same age as the rest of us.

'Hi! I'm Andy,' he said looking me in the eye. 'Nice crown.'

They all laughed. (I'd always thought I'd feel like a prat if I ended up wearing a crown for ever – but this was hardly a fashion police offence in heaven. Besides, Jesus had given it to me!)

'OK,' the blonde boy said, sitting Andy down next to me. 'Let's get some specifics. Andy, did you have weaknesses?'

'Yes, lots.'

'Give us two,' the blonde kid continued.

'Looking at dirty pictures and wanting to spend all my time playing football,' Andy said.

'So tell us what you did about it.'

'Well, I was a backsliding Christian until my sixteenth birthday. And that was the turning point for me. I wasn't happy, I knew I had to do something, so I plucked up the courage to ask one of the youth leaders at church to disciple me, and that was where it all started. I never looked back.'

'But how can football be sinful?' one of them asked.

'It's not, but I was too caught up in it. It was a passion for me. It wasn't bigger than Jesus, but it would steal my time.

The point is, I never realized it was an issue until we got well into my first year of discipleship. One Sunday we sang a song in church, which said something like "Lord, you're number one. There are no idols in my life!" And God said to me: "Good, then give up football for six months." I was absolutely gutted! That was when I realized it was a problem.'

'This sounds like… what's it called – legalism.'

'For me it was freedom,' Andy said triumphantly. 'After those six months, I enjoyed football more than ever, but it didn't have a hold on me any more. I knew I could give it up if I wanted to. I was free! I'd become obsessed with following my team as well. But God isn't too fussed about whether my team wins or loses. I mean, when someone scores a winning goal with an overhead kick, God doesn't turn to the angels and say: "Wow! Come here, lads! You've got to see this again on video!"'

Andy was good value. He was refreshing. We all took an instant liking to him. I hoped he was going to explain about the Marriage Supper, but he didn't get a chance, because the blonde-haired kid then announced to us all, 'I want you to know what happened to me back there.' He pointed to the stadium of judgement.

'I was a lukewarm Christian. I was too cool for the God Squad. I wanted to be liked. I wanted to be accepted. I wanted Jesus too, of course. Anyway, I wanted the best of both worlds, but at that judgement seat the fire turned my popularity into a small pile of dirt.

'At the judgement it was as if I was standing before Jesus saying, "Lord, your people were so embarrassing to be around and Christian stuff was so boring. Did you really expect me to give up this wonderful pile of dirt for you?"

'It was awful. I felt so ashamed standing there knowing he'd died for me.' At once we understood where the blonde-haired kid's questions had been coming from. Becky took him aside and told him what her angel had told her – how she'd never understood the grace of God properly on the old earth – how she'd never realized she was blameless, free and victorious the moment she believed.

'What about the dirty pictures?' an Asian boy asked. 'Are you talking about masturbation?'

There was no reaction to this. There was none of the embarrassment you'd expect. It was all so different here.

'Sure, total fantasy. It was stuff from the Internet, magazines, TV and films. I had to control every single avenue. Sin was stealing my joy as a Christian. I couldn't come into God's presence without having to ask him to forgive me. I was never satisfied either. Every time I looked at even very soft porn, I wanted more.

'So I gave myself rules. I only went on the Net when some-one else was in the room with me, and I never looked up at the top shelf when I entered the newsagent's. I didn't watch TV after 9 o'clock and I only watched PG- and 12-rated films.'

'Really?'

'But none of that would have made the slightest difference if I hadn't been spending time alone with God, feeding my desire for Jesus. Unless I'd been getting excited about Jesus, I'm sure I would have broken all my rules. It's all a question of being motivated by grace. As the discipleship went on, I was increasingly motivated by God's love for me. I got excited about living for him and changing the world, so I didn't want to ruin it by looking at raunchy pictures.'

'Let's just backtrack for a second,' the Asian boy said. 'You mean you wouldn't watch films, just in case they were unhelpful?'

'Exactly. The whole point was that when I got serious with God, I dealt with the "just in case".'

'But think of all the good TV programmes and films you missed, that wouldn't have done you any harm at all!'

'What about them?' Andy asked.

There was a pause. One by one we all looked round at the sparkling city walls we were about to enter. It was a question that would have seemed sensible on earth, but it sounded so stupid at the gates of heaven. Andy hadn't missed out on anything. And we all knew it.

'Besides, if I did go over the top and miss some good films, I'm sure God will let me watch them a couple of thousand times in there.' (There was more laughter as Andy pointed to the descending city, with open gates which people were massing to pour through.) 'In fact, I remember once throwing away a CD, thinking it probably was fine, but it's better to be safe than sorry!'

You couldn't argue with Andy because he was full of joy. Far from making him into a miserable killjoy, all his self-imposed rules had clearly made him happier as a red-hot Christian than he'd ever been as a lukewarm one.

One girl said, 'Andy, you're absolutely right. When I really wanted to make an impression, the hem went higher and the neckline plunged lower. I never really enjoyed the Christian life that much. And here I am now finding out how I could have done, when it's too late! So, Andy, you knew all along that Christians get judged too?'

'Yeah. It was hardly a secret, was it? There are about a hundred verses about it in the New Testament.'

'Well most of us didn't read them, or if we did, we didn't understand them,' a pretty girl said, who'd kept quiet until now. 'So what difference did knowing about the judgement make to the way you lived?'

'Well, whenever I read those passages in Corinthians about the judgement seat, I imagined myself as an old man with God asking me, "Andy, what did you do with the long life I gave you?" In fact, when I was 17, I got a calculator out and worked out that I had about 20,000 days left if I lived to old age. Seeing as I'd already blown about a thousand back-sliding, I decided to try and make the rest of them count.'

'Why didn't I think of that?' Becky said. (She'd returned with the blonde boy, whose name was Simon.)

Andy wasn't finished. He carried on, 'When I began to consider the judgement seat, it took a lot of the pressure off.'

'Really?' Becky said. 'I think it would have frightened the living daylights out of me.'

'Well, let me give you an example,' Andy continued. 'Think of all the times that people disrespect you. They're nasty, spiteful, or maybe you just get overlooked. Anyway, my natural reaction was always to resent them or more often be jealous of them. But then, when I read about the Day of Judgement, I realized that no one's going to get away with anything. That's what I mean by the pressure coming off. When I realized that all wrongs will be righted by God at judgement and that even Christians who'd done things with impure motives were going to be exposed, I just left it to God to judge them, and enjoyed life a whole lot more as a result!

'And here's the best bit: not only did I not feel jealous or resentful or aggrieved any more, I actually rather enjoyed forgiving people who'd wronged me, and I turned the other cheek because I knew I'd get rewarded for it.'

They were shocked by this.

'That's got to be wrong,' the Asian boy said. 'What, you mean you deliberately did things to earn rewards?'

'Oh yeah,' Andy replied.

'But isn't that selfish?'

'Not at all. Jesus told us to do it!'[1]

This really did come as a surprise to them.

Andy then said, 'The liberating thing about rewards is that once I'd read those verses, I wasn't bothered if people were unkind to me.[2] In fact, sometimes I found myself wanting to be especially kind to people who wouldn't be kind back.'[3]

'And what about that crown?' Becky said. 'Did you know you'd get one?'

---

1. Matthew 6 :19–20.
2. Luke 6: 32, 35.
3. Luke 14 :12–14.

'No, I didn't, but I did know that the Bible said some people were going to get rewards, and I knew that if I did get a crown, I'd want to give it to Jesus. So I didn't want to give him something plastic and tacky. I wanted to give him something awesome.'

'Let's get this straight,' someone else said. 'You deliberately tried to earn rewards?'

'Oh yeah! Big time! Jesus said, *Do not store up for yourselves treasures on earth. … But … treasures in heaven.*[1] But don't get me wrong, it wasn't my focus. My main aim was to *please him* [2] but that was because I knew I was going to appear before the judgement seat.'[3]

'What about you, Emma? You're keeping very quiet.'

I stood up and said, 'Well, I wasn't perfect, and I could have done so much more for Jesus, but whatever I did I tried to do it as if I was working for the Lord.[4] I also knew I'd get a reward for it.[5] And I'll tell you something else, I'm going in!'

With that, I stood up and started off down a slope towards the city. All of our impromptu discussion group followed. I was glad because I wanted to put them right about the martyrs and the Marriage Supper on the way. Becky was next to me.

'Do you know what it's like inside?' she asked me.

'Not exactly – I didn't have any more Bible than you.'

---

1. Matthew 6:19–20.
2. 2 Corinthians 5:9.
3. 2 Corinthians 5:10.
4. Colossians 3:23.
5. Colossians 3:24.

'What do you mean?'

'Well, until we're in heaven, we only know what the Bible tells us. But I can probably remember a few verses that might help.'

Becky said, 'I'm really getting excited now. Tell me everything you can think of about heaven. Could you give me a top ten? The angel gave me ten points about judgement – could you give me ten points to remember about heaven?'

As we moved closer and closer to the gates, I asked myself, 'What do we know about heaven?'

I began: 'Well, I don't know about a top ten, but I suppose the number one fact is that **God is there**. In heaven *the dwelling of God is with men, and he will live with them. They will be his people, and God himself will be with them and be their God.*[1]

'And because God loves us so much, **all Christians will be there**. In fact, ever since Jesus rose from the dead and ascended, he's been preparing a place for us in heaven. Jesus said, *In my Father's house are many rooms; if it were not so, I would have told you. I am going there to prepare a place for you.*[2]

We looked at the descending city. Becky said, 'I always thought that we went up to heaven.'

'Nope! This can be number three. **We don't go up to heaven. The new heaven comes down! God moves house!**'[3]

'Really? So where are we now?' Becky asked. 'Are we in a

---

1. Revelation 21:3.
2. John 14:2.
3. Revelation 21:2.

sort of limbo?'

'No, there's no such place as limbo. Every Christian goes straight from the last judgement to heaven, and, this can be your **fourth point: heaven is a place, not just a state of mind or feeling.** I mean Jesus ascended to a place not just a state of mind, didn't he![1]

'And what's more, **number five, if you like, is that we are going to see God face to face.**[2] The Bible says that on earth we only see him like a reflection in a very poor mirror.[3] But when we see him face to face, we will experience the fulfilment of every longing we've ever had, to know peace, love and utter joy.

'So, Becky, how's that for starters?'

She didn't answer. I knew why. She was bracing herself to ask her next question. I knew what it was going to be.

'Will we be able to remember our sins in heaven?' Becky asked. 'You know, I was a lukewarm Christian. Will I be eternally haunted by how rubbish I was?'

'No!'

'Are you sure?'

'Absolutely, Becky. There will be no more death or mourning or crying or pain in heaven.'[4]

'So that settles it?'

---

1. Acts 1:9–11.
2. Revelation 22:4.
3. 1 Corinthians 13:12.
4. Revelation 21:4.

'Yes, totally, because if we could remember specific sins, we might feel the pain of them. Besides, nothing impure will ever enter heaven. [1] **So we won't be able to remember specific sins. For the same reason we may not remember any friends or family who don't make it to heaven, if remembering them would make us mourn. There's no mourning in heaven. There's nothing negative at all. All that can be number six.** Just think, all through life there's always something to worry about if you really want to – now there's nothing! We're not going on holiday, forgetting our problems. Our problems have actually gone! God has dissolved them. They no longer exist. But *we* do, for ever and in heaven!'

We hugged and cried tears of joy. (We were now just about two hundred yards from the descending gates.)

'We will remember the good times, though, won't we?'

'Oh yes, we'll certainly remember God's goodness to us, because we'll want to praise him for it.'

We looked up at the city. It was so beautiful! Yet its appearance changed depending on how you looked at it.

Becky said, 'The more I stare at it, the less it looks like a city with walls surrounding it, and the more it looks like a beautiful woman dressed as a bride. Do you see what I mean?'

'Oh yes!' I replied. 'The bride symbolizes the church.'

'The church!' said Becky rather shocked, as if I'd just said a dirty word. 'Who would have thought that the church would end up marrying Jesus! But that's what's happening before

---

1. Revelation 21:27.

our very eyes, isn't it?'

I was not as surprised as Becky was to see the church looking so magnificent. I remember my old pastor telling us how much Jesus loved his church. Again and again he'd tell us that Jesus loved his church enough to die for her. He used to preach on *Christ loved the church and gave himself up for her.*[1] He used to tell us that Jesus thinks we're worth dying for, and that the church had a wonderful destiny. My old pastor was right. Now everyone could see how desirable the church was. For Becky, though, the sight of the glorious church seemed as surprising and unlikely as a glorious physics lesson!

Becky said, 'Let's make this number seven. **Christ marries his glorious bride, the church.**[2]

'Emma, it's a terrible thing to admit. But I always had a secret fear that heaven would be a bit boring. Like a never-ending church service.'

'No, it's going to be better than we expect, not worse! We know it's more wonderful and exciting than anyone's ever been able to imagine.[3] There's a verse in the Bible about some Christians who'd never seen Jesus, but were still *filled with an inexpressible and glorious joy.*[4] So seeing Jesus has got to make us feel better than that! Let's say number eight is **We are not going to be bored in heaven; we are going to be filled and**

---

1. Ephesians 5 : 25.
2. Revelation 21:2.
3. 1 Corinthians 2:9.
4. 1 Peter 1:8.

thrilled to the max! The Psalms say, *You will fill me with joy in your presence, with eternal pleasures at your right hand.*[1]

'What about married couples? Will they still be married in heaven?'

'No,' I said, 'we will be like the angels.[2] There won't be any sex in heaven either, but I'm sure there will be something better than sex.'

'Wow! Better than sex? I can't wait!'

We were now at the gates. We paused for a second. Close up we could see how the foundations of the walls were filled with beautiful jewels.[3] The gates themselves had been made out of a single pearl.[4]

'What's that writing?' Becky asked.

'Those are the names of the twelve tribes of Israel,' I answered.

'And what about the names down there at the bottom?'

'Those are the names of the twelve apostles,' I said, 'but it's not just the élite going in. People from every tribe and nation are entering.' I felt such a sense of privilege. These great walls were not fortifications to keep the devil out. He was totally absent. No, these walls stood to show that we were safe inside God's home for ever. My Christian life had taken off when I understood God's grace, and now he had delivered on all his

---

1. Psalm 16:11.
2. Luke 20:34–36.
3. Revelation 21:19.
4. Revelation 21:21.

promises to keep me by his grace and deliver me here. I had been chosen for this moment. God himself had planned that I should walk through this gateway and that made the experience so special. I said to Becky, **'Point nine: in heaven we are safe for ever.'**

We looked through the entrance into an enormous banqueting hall. There were ... I don't know ... millions inside already, and yet there were many spaces still to be filled.

'Look how bright and white they all are!' Becky said, as we gazed at the myriads of people, all of whom were dressed in white.

'Look at yourself,' I said to Becky.

She did, and looking down at her feet she was amazed to find herself clothed in a single white robe.

'Look at this!' Becky said. 'Is this really mine? Where did this come from?'

'A present from Jesus.'

Becky asked, 'Am I perfect now?'

'Yes,' I replied. 'But you've been perfect in God's eyes for ages; it's just that you never understood God's grace. Even before you were born, he planned to look at you and see Christ's perfection. You had the righteousness of Christ on the old earth – that's how you made it here! This act of being given the robe reminds us that it is a gift.'

We knelt down there and then. With the crowd all around us, we thanked God for the gift of Christ's righteousness given to us! It was such a special moment.

Becky said: 'Oh but this is the wedding supper, isn't it!

Emma, where's the seating plan? I found it hard enough talking to you. What if I'm sitting next to one of the martyrs?'

At last I had the chance to explain. 'Becky, you tell me. What did I tell you about impurity and heaven?'

Her face lit up as she said, *'Nothing impure will ever enter it!'* [1]

'So if you do sit next to a martyr, you won't be at all ashamed or jealous, because shame and jealousy are impure. And nothing impure, nothing negative can ever enter heaven. In fact, we'll be blessed when we meet these people, and their testimonies will prompt us to praise God even more.'

'We're as pure as Jesus,' Becky said. 'Thank you, Jesus!'

I was so pleased that she'd finally understood it. I added, 'Besides, when the Bridegroom enters the room, you're not going to be thinking about the other guests.'

'What do you mean?' Becky asked.

'When Jesus comes in, this place is going to go crazy!'

We held hands, and together stepped over the threshold and through the gates. Home at last!

There were lots of seats right by the entrance. We sat down on the ones nearest the door and marvelled at the sheer number of people who were still pouring in behind us.

Becky asked, 'So is everyone equal in heaven?'

I was just about to answer, when I saw someone from our old church, an old woman whose name I never knew. She hardly said boo to a goose, but I was amazed by the fuss being

---

1. Revelation 21:27.

made about her. Four angels were escorting her, past us and up to the top table close to the throne, where Jesus was surely going to sit. When she finally sat down, I saw that she was carrying a spectacularly large crown, which she placed on the table in front of her!

'Wow! Who would have thought it?' I said. 'Becky, look at that old lady. She was no one special on earth, or so we thought, but look at her reception up here.' We watched as the old lady was seated very close to Jesus' throne. Standing near her, I recognized three other faces, famous Christians – one a preacher and two worship leaders. They were in all the magazines and did those conferences. I had bought their tapes.

Then the same angels who'd seated the old lady started talking to these three men. Taking one of the celebrities by the arm, they showed him to a seat right at the back of the hall.

Becky had recognized him too. *'Many who are first will be last, and many who are last will be first,'* [1] I said.

'Does that mean he's not equal to the old lady?'

'No, we're all equal, but I think that somehow the old lady is going to have a greater capacity for reflecting God's glory. I remember my pastor once described it as the difference between a 40 watt bulb and a 100 watt bulb. Both shine fully, and the 40 watt bulb doesn't go off in a sulk because it's not a 100 watt bulb. It's perfectly happy shining away as a 40 watt bulb.'

I thought that this could be Becky's next point. So I said, **'Number ten: God loves all people equally, but one**

---

1. Matthew 19:30.

Christian may shine brighter in heaven than another.' I tried to think of the verse my pastor had used to back up his light bulbs, and then it came to me. *Those who are wise will shine like the brightness of the heavens, and those who lead many to righteousness, like the stars for ever and ever.*[1] He used to tie it in with the parable of the talents [2] where people get different degrees of reward.

Now every seat seemed to be taken. Not one was empty. A sense of anticipation built up. More spontaneous singing broke out like a Mexican wave rotating round the banqueting hall.

Then an overwhelming noise erupted. We heard what sounded like the roar of rushing waters and loud peals of thunder.[3]

This was it! Jesus had finished judging and was now following us in. He would be here any moment. We all stood, and shouted together:

Hallelujah!
    For our Lord God Almighty reigns.
Let us rejoice and be glad and give him the glory!
For the wedding of the Lamb has come,
    and his bride has made herself ready.[4]

And then a flash of light. Jesus appeared, looking even

---

1. Daniel 12:3.
2. Matthew 25:14–30.
3. Revelation 19:6.
4. Revelation 19:6–7.

more powerful and lovely than he had at the judgement. As he passed by, we all fell at his feet. Joy and excitement swept the hall as we looked at him and felt entirely satisfied. We began to celebrate, knowing that from now on, every moment would be better than the one before.

4
glorified – the christian in heaven

For those God foreknew he also predestined. ... And those he predestined, he also called; those he called, he also justified; those he justified, he also glorified. (Romans 8:29–30)

My name is Becky Mason and I am talking to you from heaven.

'What is heaven like?' you ask me.

How can I begin to describe the unending thrill of it? But I'll have a go.

Have you ever fallen in love with someone? There's an electricity you feel. Like a wave crashing over you, you are hit by something bigger than yourself. You feel out of your depth and you like it! You know what's going to happen next and you can't wait for it because you know it will feel so good. Every day is better than the best-case scenario you could ever have dreamed up for yourself. That's what it's like being with the one you love and the one who loves you. And that's what it's like being with God the Father, Son and Holy Spirit in heaven for ever.

Or put it another way: however good you might dare to think heaven will be, it is far better! Can you imagine finding God so pleasurable that every moment you long to worship him and then you satisfy that longing only for it to be renewed and satisfied again in an endless cycle of admiration?

Can you imagine all the pleasure you get from everything you most enjoy doing on earth being multiplied a million times and then bundled up into every moment of worshipping God?

Can you imagine anything that good? Well, here I am experiencing it! And all I did was believe in Jesus! I got here simply because of my faith in Jesus! And even that was a gift from God. It's the grace of God and I just want to praise him!

I don't remember what kind of Christian life I lived on the old earth. I don't remember how much or how little I did for God. All I know is that, right now, I feel full. Every sense, every part of my body, every thought is overflowing with thanks and joy at this wonderful gift given to me by God through Jesus Christ.

And when I consider the trouble he went to, to get me here! I just want to praise him again! To think that God gave up his only Son to die by crucifixion just so that I could be here!

The angels worship him too, mind you, but they're not saved sinners. They've never experienced forgiveness. They don't know what it's like to deserve hell yet end up in paradise for ever. I just cannot get over it! Jesus got the punishment we deserved on the cross, and we get heaven. What a fantastic deal!

Of course, I can't remember any sins I committed. In fact I can't remember anything negative at all. But the more I talk about what heaven's like, the more excited I get!

Anyway, I'm making it sound as if it's a one-on-one, God-and-me thing here. It's not – this is the ultimate social experience. When you get here you really appreciate other people as never before. Don't ask me to explain this, but somehow everything here is worship, and your mind is never off Jesus, whoever you're talking to or whatever you're doing. And you really see a facet of God's holiness and beauty in everyone you meet.

You probably want me to tell you what the furniture and landscape of heaven is like (and I will), but you need to understand first that when you get here, you don't think like that. Your every thought is 'Jesus'!

For example, I had the best time talking to two girls I met leaving the banqueting hall. Don't get me wrong, the Marriage Supper of the Lamb hasn't ended, but the celebrations spill out all over the place!

Anyway, let me tell you about my newest friends because they really made me want to worship Jesus. As I left the hall, the girl who was on my right was called Perpetua. Remember that name. You'll love meeting her for yourself.

Perpetua is beautiful, just like everyone else here! Let me fill you in on some of her background. She was born in North

Africa, only 180 years or so after Jesus was born in Bethlehem. She became a follower of Jesus, along with all her family except her father.

The Roman emperor had passed a law, which forbade anyone from becoming a Christian and in the year AD 202, Perpetua was arrested. She had a very young baby son at the time. Not sure how old, but she was still breastfeeding.

Perpetua told me that, before she was put on trial for being a Christian, her father came to visit her to try to persuade her to give up following Jesus. He tried every argument he could think of to change her mind. She described what happened next:

I said, 'Father do you see this waterpot lying here?'

'I see it,' he said. And I said to him, 'Can it be called by any other name than what it is?' And he answered, 'No.'

'So also I cannot call myself anything else than what I am, a Christian.'

Then my father, furious at the word 'Christian', threw himself upon me as though to pluck out my eyes …[1]

Her father had accomplished nothing. Almost immediately, Perpetua got baptized along with a handful of friends who were arrested with her. Perpetua continued:

A few days later, we were put in prison; and I was in great fear,

---

1. Robert Backhouse, *Christian Martyrs* (Hodder, 1996), p. 57.

because I had never known such darkness. What a day of horror! Terrible heat ... rough handling by the soldiers! To crown all I was tormented there by anxiety for my baby. Then my baby was brought to me and I suckled him, for he was already faint for lack of food. I obtained leave for my baby to remain in prison with me and my prison suddenly became a palace to me, and I would rather have been there than anywhere else.[1]

Perpetua's father had not given up trying to persuade her to deny Jesus. When it was rumoured that Perpetua and her friends were only a few days away from going on trial, he returned and begged her to have pity on his old age and her baby son's young life. While saying all this, he kissed her hands and fell at her feet in tears. Can you imagine?

Anyway, on the final day of the trial, Perpetua's father tried again. This time, he begged Perpetua to offer sacrifices for the welfare of the Roman emperor. (Worshipping the emperor meant denying Christ, of course.) The decisive moment of Perpetua's trial arrived, when the official in charge, called Hilarian, asked her and her friends for the last time to worship the Roman emperor. Perpetua remembers:

The procurator Hilarian said to me: 'Spare your father's white hairs; spare the tender years of your child. Offer a sacrifice for the safety of the Emperors.' And I answered, 'No.'

---

1. Backhouse, *Christian Martyrs*, p. 57.

'Are you a Christian?' said Hilarian. And I answered: 'I am.'

Then he passed sentence on all of us, and condemned us to the beasts.[1]

And so it was that on 7th March 203, Perpetua and her friends were thrown to wild animals before the crowd at an arena. An enraged cow was selected for Perpetua. The cow struck her and stunned her, until a young gladiator released her from the pain with his sword. And there she died.

As I listened to Perpetua telling her story, every detail seemed to bring glory to Jesus. She explained that this was why she could remember some of her suffering. She could not remember sin, but she could remember everything from her life which brought glory to Jesus.

Meeting Perpetua has become such a blessing to me. I have seen so much of the sweetness and steadfastness of Jesus in her.

I was even more thrilled as Perpetua told me about the diary she had written while she was in prison. To her amazement, it had been preserved and many thousands of people had turned to Jesus after reading it, especially in North Africa in the centuries that followed.

As we walked along, Perpetua introduced me to person after person who had followed Christ after reading her diary, including some from the twenty-first century! What stories they had to tell!

Perpetua and I had such fun playing games as we left the

---

1. Backhouse, *Christian Martyrs*, p. 57.

banqueting hall! My first new friend in heaven! And we've got for ever together.

I'm getting carried away! Let me tell you about my other new friend, the girl who was on my left. Her name is Cassie Bernall. She's great value!

Cassie was the same age as me, 17, when she died on 20th April 1999. She was brought up in a Christian home, but in her mid-teens things went terribly wrong. Cassie couldn't remember any specific sins, nor could she feel any of the pain of sinning against God, but she couldn't stop talking about the day Christ came into her life. From that day on, she became a bold witness for Jesus at her school, Columbine High School in Colorado, USA.

As we walked along, Cassie read me a poem she had written two days before she died:

Now I have given up on everything else
I have found it to be the only way
To really know Christ and to experience
The mighty power that brought Him back to life again,
And to find Out what it means to suffer and to Die with him,
So, whatever it takes I will be the one who lives in the fresh
Newness of life of those who are
Alive from the dead.[1]

---

1. Reproduced from Cassie Bernall's memorial service programme by permission of West Bowles Community Church, Jefferson County, Colorado, USA.

Cassie told me about what it was like being a Christian at Columbine High School. She said she'd given a videotaped testimony at her church. She had said, 'I just try to not contradict myself, to get rid of all the hypocrisy and just live for Christ.'[1]

I asked Cassie, 'So how did you die?'

'One Tuesday, I went into the school library to study Shakespeare's *Macbeth* during lunch ... you're going to find it hard to believe this ... but then two ex-students came in with guns and, well ... I got shot dead.'

Cassie told me that on the day she died she had planned to talk to some Christian friends that evening about a statement made by Martin Luther King Jr, 'If a man hasn't found something he will die for, he isn't fit to live.'[2]

She'd found the quote in a book and underlined it. She never did get to talk about it on the old earth, but she worshipped the One she lived and died for with all her energy in heaven! And what a treat it has been so far getting to know Cassie!

Cassie's life, like Perpetua's, had produced a harvest of souls. Cassie introduced me to people who'd read about her life and witness in books and newspapers, and to others who'd found Christ after reading her story on the Internet. Still others had seen her testimony on video. All had been challenged to follow Christ by Cassie's example.

---

1. *Denver Rocky Mountain News*, 27th April 1999.
2. *Denver Rocky Mountain News*, 4th June 1999.

Cassie and I rejoiced together and sang songs of praise to Jesus. Cassie loves praising Jesus! Sometimes I'd start a song, sometimes she would, and we sang duets.

As Cassie began talking to others around her, I suddenly had a flashback. Occasionally, I could remember things from my own life, but only things that prompted me to praise God.

This was a good example. I remembered a news story towards the end of my own life, about a high school shooting in America. A witness reported hearing a girl called Cassie (I think) being asked by a gunman in the school library, 'Do you believe in God?'

According to the witness, she said yes.

Then the gunman asked, 'Why?' and shot her dead.

But so far I haven't had the chance to ask Cassie what exactly happened in that school library, because as I was about to, something awesome happened. We emerged from the huge banqueting hall and looked up. On the horizon we saw something that took our breath away. I'd tried to imagine it as a child. Now Cassie and I were seeing God's throne. There it was, shining bright. And from the throne, a beautifully clear river flowed towards us! [1]

Everyone around me gasped as we looked at the throne. I ran towards it and dived into the river. Splashing my way towards the throne, I started drinking the water. Except, it wasn't water at all – it was sweeter and more satisfying than any other drink. I gulped it in as we were carried away by the

---

1. Revelation 22:1–2.

river's current.[1] It was such fun! I span out of the water onto the bank and looked on towards the throne in admiration. Next to me on the bank was an angel who was laughing heartily as we all enjoyed ourselves.

'Can you tell me more about heaven?' I asked him.

'How long have you got?' he asked back. We both laughed again.

'Can we approach the throne together?' I asked.

'Sure.'

'And can I ask you more about heaven as we go?'

'Of course,' the angel replied, seeming genuinely pleased at the idea. And why not?

'How about this,' I continued, flushed with enthusiasm. 'Every time you tell me something about heaven, I'll worship God for it! In fact I'll make up a song about it.' I loved the music of heaven; it was so much better than music on the old earth, and I seemed to have a spontaneous ability to create it here. New songs flowed continually from deep within me. I could never carry a tune on the old earth, but here I loved it!

'OK, let's sing about this,' the angel said. 'This is a place where the desire to lose yourself in worship never fades. And **the first thing about heaven has got to be that the Lord God Almighty and the Lamb are the focus of thrilling worship.** Some Christians on the old earth secretly feared that they'd spend eternity on a boring solitary cloud plucking a harp. Others thought that heaven would be like a church

---

1. Revelation 21:6.

service that never ends. How wrong they were!'

The angel went on: 'The glory of God in its fullness cannot be contained in a building or a meeting. It's grander than that! We don't go into a temple or building to worship our King here,[1] because we are in his presence to the uttermost every moment.'

It was too much, too fast. I wanted the angel to slow down. 'What do you mean?' I asked.

'Well, for example, in the Bible we read that people who were exposed to the glory of God wanted to die because they were sinful. Here people not only survive God's presence, but they thoroughly enjoy it! Here you have the capacity to reflect his glory perfectly. Rather than wanting to die, you want more and more of him. And you bounce back rays of glory to his throne. He is the source of all the light and life you enjoy.'

'And this is all in the Bible, is it?'

'Absolutely, *The city does not need the sun or the moon to shine on it, for the glory of God gives it light, and the Lamb is its lamp.*[2] There's no night or darkness here.[3] The good times never stop. You're not idle; you're constantly serving him,[4] but you're never worn out. You're continually re-energized by his beauty and closeness.'

---

1. Revelation 21:22.
2. Revelation 21:23.
3. Revelation 21:25.
4. Revelation 22:3.

I burst into a new song thanking God for all of this. But my mind was still working overtime. When I finished singing, I had another drink from the river of life. I asked the angel, 'What about streets of gold and pearly gates?'

'Everyone asks that!' the angel replied. 'All these phrases in the Bible symbolize something better and more wonderful than words can convey. The Bible actually says that the great street of the city is made of *pure gold, like transparent glass.*[1] Now you know that you can't see through pure gold. No, gold symbolizes the preciousness of God himself and transparency represents his purity and holiness. Take a look!'

The angel gestured towards the great street of the city. As I looked for golden streets, the very fabric of heaven throbbed with God's purity and holiness, just like the angel said! I looked and just knew that this was a symbol, which only began to touch the depths of the glory it represented. Every symbol I saw was a pale reflection of something far more glorious.

The angel said: 'This is what God has prepared for those he loves!'

Repeating some of the lyrics of the songs the angel and I had been singing, he went on, **'We'll make your song about "the Lord is heaven's light" song number two. And one about "the river of life" being a "sweet taste of God's abundant love from his throne" can be number three.**

'It's all free grace and there's lots of it,' the angel said,

---

1. Revelation 21:21.

throwing me into the water again! As my head bobbed up, he shouted in triumph, 'Jesus said, *To him who is thirsty I will give to drink without cost from the spring of the water of life.*' [1]

In the river itself, I was more aware than ever before of God's abundant grace. He'd done nothing by half measures. On the contrary, everything was served with lashings of ice cream and custard up here!

As someone else larking around in the river put it, 'First we realize that he has lavished the riches of his grace on us [2] and we get excited about that. But then we wonder, "Why did he bother to save us in the first place?" We then realize that he's saved us simply because he wanted to show us the *incomparable riches of his grace, expressed in his kindness to us in Christ Jesus.*' [3]

Now that really is awesome! He saved us because he wants us to enjoy this incomparable grace for ever!

The angel fished me out of the river and we walked on beside the bank towards the throne. We sang and worshipped as we went, and other worshippers joined us. 'Now you tell me,' the angel asked, 'what else do you notice here?'

What a question! There was so much to see. Rolling hills, heavenly weather, open country and then again, round the corner, all the home comforts of city life, awesome buildings and stunning architecture. All of it seemed to inspire worship.

---

1. Revelation 21:6.
2. Ephesians 1:8.
3. Ephesians 2:7.

There was a grandeur about it all.

After a moment's reflection, the theme of a fourth new song came to me. **'There's no separation in heaven,'** I sang. The song was all about how we were in harmony with our God and each other and our surroundings.

The angel said, 'That's right, there's *no longer any sea*[1] and sea represents separation in the book of Revelation.'

No separation. How wonderful to say 'hello' but never wave goodbye, I thought.

'What else?' the angel asked.

I looked ahead at the throne and at the ecstatically happy worshippers dancing towards it. 'There's an atmosphere here which is a mixture of relief and sheer pleasure coming together in celebration and worship! We've won! And there's our champion!' I shouted, knees pumping and charging towards Jesus at the centre of the throne.

'It's all over!' yelled one delirious merrymaker who skipped past us, arms aloft worshipping his King. That summed it up nicely.

It is all over! All the worries and stress of life are gone. We made this track five on our heavenly CD journey towards the throne.

I sang:

> From now on,
> No worries.
> No stress.

---

1. Revelation 21:1.

No deadlines.

No people or situations to avoid.

Nothing lurking in the back of my mind.

Nothing to escape from or wish away.

And no regrets.

From now on, no pressure.

I am totally fulfilled.

I was so fascinated by this line of thinking that, just for fun, I got some revellers nearby to join us in a game. We started a list of people who'd be out of work in heaven. Here it is.

People who'll need to retrain beyond the grave include prison and police officers, surgeons, doctors, nurses and undertakers, everyone who works in homeless shelters and orphanages, everyone involved in famine and disaster relief, and, of course, evangelists – everyone up here's already a Christian!

The angel shouted triumphantly, 'It's all over! He is *the Alpha and the Omega, the beginning and the end.*[1] And this is the end. This is the time where God himself *will wipe away every tear from their eyes. There will be no more death or mourning or crying or pain, for the old order of things has passed away.*'[2]

With each step forward, the worship around the throne became more intoxicating. We picked up the pace as we neared the masses surrounding Jesus, the Lamb at the centre of the throne.

---

1. Revelation 21:6.
2. Revelation 21:4.

'What shall we sing about next?' the angel asked me.

'It's so safe here and I feel so at home!' I replied, making a mental note that this was our sixth song, I think.

'Of course you do,' the angel said. 'Your citizenship is in heaven.[1] You were always a stranger on the old earth.[2] That's why you feel at home here.'

This was so true. The angel explained to me that in the Bible, the number twelve means completeness. So when Revelation 21:17 says that the walls are '144 cubits thick', it's picture language explaining that everyone who's supposed to be here has made it inside the walls. The city itself is described as being a perfect cube in its measurements, 12,000 units in width, height and length. But I felt perfectly safe in the city, not because of its massive size or impenetrable walls. No, I was eternally safe knowing that God had brought his chosen people to a perfect heaven. And I was in! Saved by grace through faith in Jesus Christ!

I was learning fast. 'Tell me about those trees,' I said to the angel, pointing out two stupendous trees either side of the river, each of which had the most fantastic fruit growing from them.

'No, you tell me about them,' the angel replied.

'What do you mean?'

'Well, think Bible, and think tree!'

'You mean the tree of life in the Garden of Eden?' I asked

---

1. Philippians 3:20.
2. 1 Peter 1:1.

rather hesitantly. (You've got to bear in mind that when you arrive in heaven, God doesn't instantly download all knowledge from his hard drive onto the floppy disk of your brain. That would make it boring! As you can tell, we're constantly making new discoveries up here, which is half the fun of it!)

'OK,' the angel continued, 'so mankind started in Eden with a tree. And this is where you end up with another tree. Remember also that when Adam and Eve ate from that tree a curse came upon them and their descendants. Yet the Bible says that that curse never enters heaven.[1] So think about it,' the angel said. 'Before Adam and Eve took that apple, there was no death or suffering, the dwelling of God was with his people, creation was perfect.'

Someone nearby butted in, 'So that was paradise lost, and this is paradise regained! After all, there's no death or suffering here. Here the dwelling of God is with us, we've got the tree of life, and the curse has been removed. And creation looks more beautiful here than it ever did on the old earth. We're back to Eden – paradise regained.'

'In fact,' I said, 'it's better than that. We're not just back where we started. Adam and Eve lived in a world that was smashed by sin, but this paradise can never be broken.[2] Besides, Adam and Eve had no concept of being sinners saved by grace!'

'Heaven is better than paradise in Eden' was my seventh song. Talk about quality of life!

---

1. Revelation 22:3.
2. Revelation 21:4.

I looked back at the tree. Hmmn ... That fruit did look a bit special. Much more attractive than you could ever imagine food to be. I really wanted some. 'Hey, Mr Angel,' I said, 'I might be bang out of order even to ask you this, but I don't suppose there's any chance I could have a little bite out of some of that fruit?'

The angel replied, 'Now that is a silly question!'

'Thought so,' I said. 'It was probably a non-starter, but it just looks so good that ...'

The angel interrupted, 'Eat all you want!'

'You mean that I can eat from the tree of life?'

'Of course you can. What do you think the fruit is for? It's for you to enjoy! After Adam and Eve got kicked out of the garden, the tree was guarded by a flaming sword flashing back and forth,[1] but there's nothing to stop you here – in fact you are positively encouraged to eat up! And you can come back again and again and again, because this tree will never stop bearing fruit.'[2]

I sank my teeth into an apple. It was delicious. And guess what? No side effects! I then had all kinds of other fruits I'd never seen before. With each mouthful, I felt total satisfaction and extreme pleasure. And there was more than enough for everyone. We lacked nothing.

Sharing the fruit around, we punched the air and broke into yet more praise. In a mass bundle, someone grabbed me

---

1. Genesis 3:24.
2. Revelation 22:2.

by the ankles and, lifting me off the ground, twirled me round like a baton. With my hands outstretched I screamed with excitement as heaven's golden country whizzed by. He let me go like a discus thrower and I spiralled up and then bombed down into the river. Climbing out, delirious, I ran after the guy who'd chucked me in. But I couldn't catch him. Then he jumped out from behind one of the trees, and looked me square in the eye.

I stopped in my tracks. Something in this young man's chiselled face was familiar. He stood still, beaming a smile.

'Richard?' I said, not believing my eyes. 'Is it really you?'

'Of course it is, Becky.'

I looked at a broad-shouldered, strapping young man. His physique was superb. He looked like an Olympic sprinter or prizefighter entering the ring. He was wearing a single robe, draped over one shoulder. His other shoulder was bare sculptured muscle. He had a noble bearing, like some warrior of old. His face was marvellously handsome, and yet unmistakably, something about him reminded me of my cousin Richard, who had been born with Down's syndrome.

I couldn't deny it. This magnificently beautiful man had the same cheeky grin, the same playful eyes, as my cousin, for whom much of life had been a struggle. Was this really Richard with face, body and speech transformed?

'Richard Mason?' I said still unsure. 'Where did I take you on Saturdays?'

'To the park to play on the swings.'

'And who's Richard's favourite cousin?'

'Boomper!' he shouted, which is what he always called me! But it was amazing hearing him shout it so clearly.

We hugged for I don't know how long! Richard had died aged 14, but not before a simple trust in Jesus had blossomed in his heart. Now he was gloriously changed.

'Come and meet the others!' Richard said, and without waiting for a reply he ran off. 'Who were the others?' I wondered. I gave chase. His bare feet thudded into the turf in front of me. His huge calf muscles pounded him forward at enormous speed. We dashed through a forest, and then, lean-ing into a corner, a clearing swung into view ahead of us. And then I heard a great cheer: 'Welcome home, Becky!'

My family! Tears of joy flooded out as I ran straight into my grandad's arms. There was Grandma, Mum and Dad and wherever I looked, friends and family. What a reunion! They all stood round in a circle, and I embraced one after another. My uncle John told me how he was going to take me out sailing; Auntie Pam wanted to get us all round the piano, just like at Christmas time. My cousins Andy, Kate and Sarah wanted me to play tennis. 'But not just us,' Kate said. 'Thousands come to watch us, just like we always hoped they would.' Sarah pointed towards a mountain range. 'First let's go ski-ing,' she said.

They told me they didn't spend literally every moment standing around the throne, with feet rooted to the spot. Kate said, 'It's so wonderful, Becky. After we've enjoyed one activity, it's as if God says, "How have you enjoyed it so far?" We reply, "It's the best thing ever," and then God says, "Oh no it's not! I've got something far better to show you. Come over here." And the same process is repeated again and again. Yet all our service and activity here is the same as our worship around the throne! It's all for God's glory!'

It made sense that God wanted us to enjoy and explore the heaven he'd made for us. As a family we sang:

> *You are worthy, our Lord and God,*
> *to receive glory and honour and power,*
> *for you created all things,*
> *and by your will they were created*
> *and have their being.* [1]

What a family reunion heaven had turned out to be! Every precious memory I had of family and friends was exceeded. 'And this is just the start!' my cousin Andy said. 'Wait until you meet the heroes of the Bible and of all the centuries.'

Had I ever doubted that such a marvellous homecoming awaited me in heaven? Perhaps I had. But now we were together in a worshipful celebration of Jesus that would never end. Much later, after many joyous conversations, I found my cousin Richard again. What a sight he was!

Personally speaking, I'd never liked the way I looked on the old earth. In fact, the only part of my body I was ever happy with were my teeth! Now I was … perfect! Stunning actually, if I do say so myself! When I thought of the most beautiful

---

1. Revelation 4:11.

person I'd seen on the old earth, I realized that everyone here was better looking than that! And who better than Richard to ask all about it!

'We all get new bodies,' he said. 'It's no secret. The Bible tells us again and again. After we died, our bodies got burned or buried. But when Jesus returned to earth, God somehow found a tiny molecule or seed of what was left. And God used that seed to grow us splendid new bodies. My old body was affected by Down's syndrome. It eventually gave up on me because it was perishable, but my new body is *raised imperishable*. My old body was *sown in dishonour*, but my new one is *raised in glory*; my old body was *sown in weakness*, but now it's been *raised in power*.[1] For me, Becky, this is a dream come true!'

'For me too, mate!' I thought. But Richard was desperate to tell me something else.

'Look over there, next to your uncle John.'

I saw a guy I didn't recognize, dressed in a robe like Richard's.

'That's a distant relative or descendant we never met on the old earth. Anyway, his name's Paul.'

'And …'

'Well,' Richard continued, obviously bursting with excitement, 'he was alive on earth, when Jesus returned.'

'Really?'

'Big time.'

'So what happened to him?'

---

1. 1 Corinthians 15:43.

'Ask him yourself!' Richard replied.

I walked over to Paul who embraced me like a long-lost sister. 'Paul, tell me about it!' I said. 'What was it like seeing Jesus return to earth?'

'Well,' Paul replied, 'it was deafening and very exciting. First, Jesus himself came down from heaven *with a loud command, with the voice of the archangel and with the trumpet call of God.*[1] And the bodies of all the believers who'd already died were resurrected first. After that all of us believers who were still alive were *caught up together with them in the clouds to meet the Lord in the air.*'[2]

'Awesome!' I said. But before I could ask anything else, Richard grabbed us both by the arm. My family and friends were all off, up and running towards the throne, still in view ahead of us. We wanted to go with them, so we set off after them.

The angel I'd been with fell in beside me. We ran but never felt breathless!

'Hi Becky! Found anything else to sing about?'

'Lots,' I answered, feeling sky high! 'I've just met my family. Then … oh yeah … **my eighth song was about how everyone gets a new body in heaven**, and then I met someone who was alive on earth when Jesus returned.'

'Who else do you want to meet?' the angel asked as we sprinted along.

What a lovely question! Could I really meet everyone and

---

1. 1 Thessalonians 4:16.
2. 1 Thessalonians 4:17.

anyone who'd ever believed? Could I really quiz saints from all time? Was this really a fantasy of time travel and timelessness come true? Before I could draw up my list, I wanted to ask the angel something else.

'I just met my family, but it didn't seem weird to be able to recognize each other. Should I have been surprised? Does the Bible say we'll be able to recognize each other up here?'

'Not exactly, but there are some big clues. For example, the disciples recognized the risen Jesus and he recognized them. And the disciples recognized Moses and Elijah when they appeared on a mountain with Jesus.'[1]

The more I thought about it, I realized that eternal life would be meaningless if I didn't know who I was. And so it wasn't that much of a surprise that other people knew who I was, and welcomed me home! Once again, heaven had turned out to be better than my wildest dreams.

But it wasn't a dream. My body was real enough and the ground underfoot was solid. I asked the angel as we ran on, 'Where exactly are we? Is this heaven or earth?'

'It's ... er ...both!' he replied. 'God has made a new heaven and a new earth[2] and joined them together so you can go from one to the other without noticing the difference. The old earth you lived on was burned,[3] but now God has renewed it just like the Bible promised.'[4]

---

1. Matthew 17:2–3.
2. Revelation 21:1; 2 Peter 3:13.
3. 2 Peter 3:7–10.
4. Romans 8:19–21.

I sang a new song, my ninth new song, praising God for renewing the earth and joining it to a new heaven. I sang, 'Lord, you make all things new!' [1]

All this time, the angel and I had been approaching God's throne. We had now arrived. But I really felt my life was just beginning. It had all been just shadows on the old earth. This was real life gazing into the wonderful eyes of my Father. Despite all the others there, as I looked at my heavenly Father, he seemed to be looking straight at me. It was a look that said, 'You are adopted, and accepted and you are mine.' He was so warm and loving, yet big and powerful at the same time.

Thousands of others fell in behind me as the massive crowd swelled. Yet everywhere we went in heaven and whatever we did, we seemed just as close to him as this.

What is it like to see God? Well, from first glance you get overwhelmed by his holiness. This holiness is not just the absence of sin – it's the positive presence of someone who is ultimately holy.

Then we heard singing:

> *Holy, holy, holy*
> *is the Lord God Almighty,*
> *who was, and is, and is to come.* [2]

God's holiness is so powerful. In fact everything here is holy. How wonderful it was to be totally pure, and to look at

---

1. Revelation 21:5.
2. Revelation 4:8.

total purity. [1] How wonderful to be glorified in the presence of our glorious creator!

As I looked, *I saw a Lamb, looking as if it had been slain, standing in the centre of the throne.* [2]

The Lamb was Jesus, my slain Saviour, and there was an expression of joy on his face. I looked again and the Lamb appeared as victor returning from the field of conquest. He was *dressed in a robe reaching down to his feet and with a golden sash round his chest. His head and hair were white like wool, as white as snow, and his eyes were like blazing fire. His feet were like bronze glowing in a furnace, and his voice was like the sound of rushing waters.* [3]

He seemed about to speak. *His face was like the sun shining in all its brilliance.* [4] And then he said, *I am the First and the Last. I am the Living One; I was dead, and behold I am alive for ever and ever!* [5]

I sang my tenth song: 'In heaven, death is defeated and life is eternal.' Jesus has beaten death. This life will never end. Nothing can stop me doing what I long to do, which is to worship the King of kings and Lord of lords!

The angel said to me, 'Think about it: raised to life, in the Lord's constant presence, on a renewed earth which is the

---

1. 1 John 3:2.
2. Revelation 5:6.
3. Revelation 1:13–15.
4. Revelation 1:16.
5. Revelation 1:18.

home of righteousness,[1] with no tears, pain, disease or death. And *we will be with the Lord for ever.'*[2]

'And that's just for starters,' I said laughing to myself. After this, I looked –

and there before me was a great multitude that no-one could count, from every nation, tribe, people and language, standing before the throne and in front of the Lamb. They were wearing white robes and were holding palm branches in their hands. And they cried in a loud voice:

> *'Salvation belongs to our God,*
> *who sits on the throne*
> *and to the Lamb.'*[3]

What a scene of rejoicing! How can I begin to describe it to you? The Bible says that there is joy in heaven over one sinner who repents. Think of how noisy it gets when we all go steaming in! And what a scene of wonder! If the presence of Jesus on earth in the first century inspired worship, and the giving of the Holy Spirit caused Christian hearts to thrill, think what it is like to be in the presence of God, the entire Trinity face to face!

As the excitement built, flashes of lightning flew out from

1. 2 Peter 3:13.
2. 1 Thessalonians 4:17.
3. Revelation 7:9–10.

the throne, along with rumblings and peals of thunder. [1] Now a momentum was gathering. The noise increased and the angels cried out:

> *Worthy is the Lamb, who was slain,*
> *to receive power and wealth and wisdom and strength*
> *and honour and glory and praise!* [2]

Then a new wave of gratitude crashed into our hearts. I heard every creature singing even more loudly:

> *To him who sits on the throne and to the Lamb*
> *be praise and honour and glory and power,*
>   *for ever and ever!* [3]

And I sang too. I have never felt as good as I do now in his presence. Come on, join me!

---

1. Revelation 4:5.
2. Revelation 5:12.
3. Revelation 5:13.

what next?

Will you be there around the throne of God?

A Christian can say yes. A Christian can say, 'I'm sure I'll be in heaven; I know it for a fact.' Are you sure you're going to heaven? Do you have that certainty?

If you're not sure, then you can be, but following Jesus is a big commitment and involves a real cost.

To become a Christian, you need to do three things:

1. Say 'Sorry' – Tell God you're sorry for the wrong things you've done.
2. Say 'Thank you' – Thank God for punishing Jesus rather than you for those wrong things.
3. Say 'Please' – Ask God to come into your life as you follow Jesus Christ.

If you are serious about living for God, then you could pray this prayer:

Dear God,

I'm really sorry for everything I've done wrong. [Name some specifics.] I turn away from all those things, and I understand that by praying this prayer, I will never have to do any of those things again.

Thank you for sending Jesus into the world to take the punishment I should have got for what I've done wrong. Thank you that Jesus died as my substitute. Thank you that I can know that I'm now totally forgiven, because all my sin has been completely taken by Jesus instead of me.

Please come into my life now as I commit myself to following Jesus, whatever it takes and whatever the cost. Amen.

If you've prayed this prayer and meant it, you really need to tell someone who is a Christian today – or tomorrow at the latest – so that they can help you further.

And please tell me too! You can email me at

adrian_ holloway@hotmail.com

Or if you want to, you can write to me at

    Adrian Holloway
    Oasis Church
    30 Acacia Road, Bournville, Birmingham B30 2AL

There is also a website for you to explore, which will help you wrestle with some of the questions you may have – and lots more besides. The site address can be found on the back cover of this book.

now read this . . .

There's some Bible teaching that's not explained in Chapters 1–4. In a short book, by emphasizing some doctrines, I have inevitably underemphasized others. I did this deliberately because I was determined to write a short book aimed at people who would never read a long book about anything, especially religion!

The intermediate state

For example, in seeking to emphasize that *man is destined to die once, and after that to face judgment* (Hebrews 9:27), I have said nothing about what the Bible says happens to us in between death and judgement. The Bible does not teach that when we die we go straight to the final judgement. Neither does the Bible teach that when we die we experience 'soul sleep', during which we're not conscious of anything until we're woken up by the final judgement.

In fact, the Bible teaches that after death, Christians are immediately in the presence of the Lord. This was certainly

Paul's expectation (2 Corinthians 5:8; Philippians 1:23). And Jesus himself promised the thief on the cross, *I tell you the truth, today you will be with me in paradise* (Luke 23:43). Some theologians have therefore called this state 'paradise' rather than 'heaven'. Whichever term is preferred, all Christians can be sure that they will be with the Lord immediately after death. (In fact, in Revelation 6:9 we seem to be reading about dead Christians who are in heaven before the final judgement.) Theologians call this period after death but before judgement 'the intermediate state'.

What happens to non-Christians during this intermediate state? Looking back through this book, you will find a clue in the story of the rich man and Lazarus, which I have reproduced in Chapter 1 (pp. 36–38).

I have located the suffering of the rich man *in hell* (Luke 16:23), that is, after the final judgement. Actually, in the original Greek text, Jesus says the rich man is suffering in a place called 'Hades', which is a Greek word used elsewhere in the New Testament to describe the intermediate state after death but before the final judgement.

By the time Jesus came to earth, it seems that Jews had developed a view that Hades had two parts: a good part, which we might call 'paradise', where Lazarus was, and a bad part, where the rich man was.

If we take this view, we need to ask what happens to people in the bad part of Hades at the final judgement. Revelation 20:13–14 (which you'll find in Chapter 1 p. 17) provides the answer. *Death and Hades gave up the dead that were in them,*

and each person was judged according to what he had done.
Then death and Hades were thrown into the lake of fire. The
lake of fire is the second death (Revelation 20:13–14). The
impression given here and elsewhere in the New Testament is
that those in the bad part of Hades go from bad to worse
when they are thrown into hell, and that their final state is
worse than their intermediate state.

It is therefore sobering to think that the rich man suffers
torment (Luke 16:23) and *agony* (Luke 16:24) in Hades. It
may be that Jesus is giving us a good idea of what hell will be
like for the rich man.

You may find this diagram helpful.[1] It is a very simplified

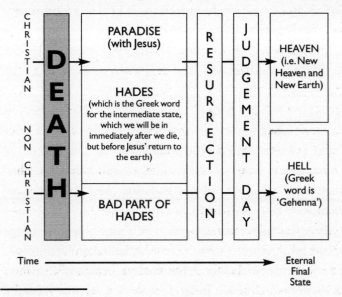

---

1. Freely adapted from *Heaven ... it's not the end of the world* by David
   Lawrence (Scripture Union, 1995).

view of the New Testament's teaching about what happens to us when we die.

If we are consciously in God's presence in the good part of Hades, or without his comfort in the bad part of Hades immediately after death, you might think that Christ's verdict on us at the final judgement will actually come as no big surprise to anyone. After all, we'll have had a taste during the intermediate state of what's coming to us later. However, this kind of thinking hardly does justice to the numerous New Testament passages that present Judgement Day as a fearsome day of surprises and shocks (e.g. Matthew 7:21–23; Matthew 11:22–23; Matthew 25:31–46; Luke 8:17; Luke 12:2–3; Romans 2:16; 1 Corinthians 3:12–15; 1 Corinthians 4:5). This book is an attempt to do justice to these scriptures, and, as I have said above, other doctrines have been relatively overlooked as a result.

The Millennium

This is a case in point. In the book I make no mention of the thousand-year reign of Christ on the earth before the final judgement, which is what Revelation 20:1–10 has been understood by many Christians to mean.

There is considerable disagreement about how this passage should be interpreted, and one view, called amillennialism, does not anticipate a literal thousand-year reign of Christ on the earth before the last judgement at all. I suppose my book is therefore amillennial. But here necessity rather than conviction is the reason for the omission. I have deliberately written a short book designed to arouse curiosity about what the Bible teaches. With more material than space, I had to be selective, and a detailed consideration of Revelation 20:1–10 was excluded on that basis alone.

Finally, it is of course impossible for anyone at the final judgement to be sent back to life as we know it today (as Daniel was towards the end of Chapter 1). The final judgement is final. It takes place after the world and life as we know it have been brought to an end by Christ's return to earth. *Man is destined to die once, and after that to face judgment* (Hebrews 9:27).

But no one who has read this book will ever be able to say they were not warned. And no one who has read this book need ever experience the shock of their lives beyond death.

Rather than shocks, Jesus offers you abundant life, if you will follow him. He says, *I have come that they may have life, and have it to the full* (John 10:10).

Will you follow him?

QUESTIONS FOR REFLECTION
AND DISCUSSION

Try to find a question that helps you (or your group) to think
and talk about the issues that concern you.

1

horrified - the non-christian

1. What would happen to you if you died today? Has reading this chapter changed your view in any way?

2. How did you feel as you read about (a) the queue; (b) the books recording people's lives, including your life; (c) the lake of fire?

3. How much did you know about Jesus before you read this chapter? Do you understand anything differently now?

4. Do you think that God is fair in sending people to hell?

5. Do you think God was unfair to punish his innocent Son?

6. What would you now want to tell people (a) in the church, and (b) outside the church about the reality of hell?

2

gutted - the lukewarm christian

1. Do you think you will have anything of value to offer Jesus when you stand before him at his judgement seat?

2. How do you feel about lapsed (failed) Christians being allowed into heaven, when good people go to hell?

3. Have you decided to live any differently since reading this chapter?

4. How hard do you find it to leave God to judge others and not worry about how they treat you?

5. Is there someone you want to talk to about Jesus right now?

6. If God decides who goes to heaven and who doesn't, why do we have to tell people about Jesus?

3

ecstatic - the red-hot christian

1. Would you say that you were looking forward to dying and being with Jesus?

2. Do you find that people's opposition puts you off living openly for Jesus?

3. Can you identify with Emma when she talks about the grace of God changing the way she lived? And with Andy when he talked about giving himself rules to keep away from temptation?

4. If you had your time over again, would you do anything differently?

5. Do you think it's right to be motivated by the thought of rewards in heaven?

4

glorified - the christian in heaven

1. How did you imagine heaven before reading this chapter? Has your view changed at all?

2. Is there anyone from the past or the present day that you are particularly looking forward to meeting in heaven?

3. What are you most looking forward to leaving behind when you go to heaven?

4. Which would you regard more as the shock of your life – to go to hell, or to go to heaven?